A to Z

of

LEASING & ASSET FINANCE

Julian Rose & Stephen Bassett

First published as a hardback original in 2017

This third edition published in 2024

Copyright © Julian Rose & Stephen Bassett

The moral right of this author has been asserted.

All rights reserved.

No part of this publication may be reproduced, stored in a retrieval system, or transmitted, in any form or by any means, without the prior permission in writing of the publisher, nor be otherwise circulated in any form of binding or cover other than that in which it is published and without a similar condition including this condition being imposed on the subsequent purchaser.

Design, typesetting and publishing by UK Book Publishing

www.ukbookpublishing.com

ISBN: 978-1-917329-29-3

CONTENTS

Acknowledgements	1
Foreword	2
Introduction	4
What is Leasing?	6
History	8
A-Z of Terms	12
Index	198
Abbreviations	209
Select Bibliography	212
Asset Finance 50	213
Request for Input	217
About the Authors	218

ACKNOWLEDGEMENTS

Mark Jones, Jason Lekerman, Rob Morris-Jones, Neil Ryan, Roger Skinner, Robert Taylor and Helena Thernstrom kindly suggested content for this edition or reviewed certain terms.

The authors are also grateful to readers of the first and second editions for their comments and suggestions. Any errors or omissions are the sole responsibility of the authors.

FOREWORD

What is a Lease? Obvious, you might say. Yet, in my experience it doesn't have to be.

The meaning of a word is dependent on its context.

As a junior lawyer working for an international asset finance company, I often found myself drafting agreements trying to put on paper how a business relationship was intended to work. The negotiations were long and complex, agreements spilling out over pages and pages. All too often, there would be a moment when the parties got stuck, could not understand the other side and could not see a way forward. Many times, this was because of differing interpretations of a clause or a word. By scaling it back to the exact sentence or word and seeking agreement on how it should be understood, negotiations got unstuck and a solution could be found.

I learned the value of the basic question 'exactly what do you mean by that?'. I also learned that disputes are only a short step away from a simple misunderstanding.

In an AI powered world where detail might be sacrificed in the name of speed, it is even more important to seek clarity of definitions. As my MS Copilot itself puts it: 'AI can be a threat to nuanced understanding of words, as it can often rely on statistical patterns, algorithms, or predefined rules, rather than on the contextual, intentional, and interpretive aspects of human communication.'

The word lease might mean one thing to one thing to a Brit and a different thing to an American, one thing to a lawyer and a different thing to an accountant, one thing to a tenant and a different thing to a car dealership.

Earlier in the year I took over as Chair of the Leasing Foundation. In this role I have had the privilege to have several interesting conversations with people from across our industry. My question to all of them has been 'what do you think the purpose of the foundation should be?'. The answers have all revolved around words like collaboration and community. In a world seemingly dominated by division and polarisation, we seek understanding and shared goals.

Understanding each other is easier if communication is built on common terminology.

The A - Z of Leasing and Asset Finance is an essential tool for all of us, both long term members of this field and those just embarking on their career. The copies we have in the Simply office are in high demand. It is a shortcut to understanding our industry and has over the years earned its place in all training programmes and talent development initiatives of substance. This edition reflects the changing times, with new terms added and others updated.

To anyone navigating the complexities of leasing and asset finance, whether you are an existing or a future leader of this industry, keep a copy of this book within reach. It will be of use.

Ylva Oertengren
Chief Operating Office, Simply Asset Finance
Chair, The Leasing Foundation
July 2024

INTRODUCTION

This A-Z of Leasing and Asset Finance explains the key concepts and techniques of this vital and significant part of the UK business finance market.

The scope of the book spans the business and financial services environment in which the industry sits; the asset finance and leasing market and how it operates; trade bodies, regulators and other official bodies; the variety of agreement types which exist and the general legal and regulatory frameworks surrounding such agreements.

It is designed to assist everybody: from individuals within leasing companies; finance brokers; equipment suppliers and dealers who offer asset finance options; as well as those in the wider financial services market (including banks) who need to understand leasing solutions. It can also provide a valuable overview to those who are new to the market and a useful up-to-date reference guide for established practitioners.

The scope is framed as widely as possible. It encompasses any arrangements by which a finance company provides to another party a bailment, or the right of use, of the equipment or vehicles that it owns, under an agreement made between them.

The explanations describe the various ways in which some terms are used for different purposes, including for accounting, taxation, and in law and regulation.

Each definition is linked using *#hashtags* to one or more of twenty topics, spanning the business and financial services environment in which the industry operates, leasing operations, and the relevant legal and regulatory frameworks. The Index is sorted by topics, allowing the reader to review all associated terms together.

Many of the definitions use other terms in the book. Where the cross-reference provides key context, the first word of the associated term is capitalised.

All entries were prepared using the latest available information in Summer 2024.

Despite great care being taken, there will inevitably be errors and omissions for which the authors accept full responsibility. Comments from readers will be very welcome and will be used to continually update, improve and refine the book in future editions.

WHAT IS LEASING?

Of all the terms in this book, perhaps one of the most difficult to define is the most fundamental one, i.e. 'leasing'. It is of such importance to the other terms in the book that it is repeated here.

Leasing is not a term specifically defined in law. It is defined in accounting regulations, but not in other areas of regulation (that tend to cross-refer to the accounting regulation),

In law, a leasing contract is seen as a relationship of 'bailment', meaning there is a temporary transfer of assets from one person to another. Similarly, for accounting purposes under international accounting rules, a leasing contract gives the 'right of use' of an asset to another person.

So is any contract of 'bailment' in law, or one that provides the 'right of use' for accounting purposes, leasing? Generally, yes, but with certain refinements:

- In common use of the term 'leasing' it is usual to exclude short-term rentals from the definition of the leasing market. There is no clear line, but bailments of less than 12 months are generally considered to be part of the short-term rental market rather than leases. Under the new international lease accounting standard, IFRS 16, lessees have the option not to report leases of less than 12 months on their balance sheets.
- It is common to focus on business, rather than individual consumer, leasing when discussing the leasing market, with the term 'hire' being more common in the consumer market. But this is changing, as leasing becomes more relevant to consumers as we move to a more sustainable, circular economy.

There are a host of different bailment arrangements in common use. Some include the word 'lease', others do not - such as hire purchase and conditional sale. For accounting and tax purposes, they are all likely to be categorised as leases.

The term 'asset finance' is often assumed to be synonymous with 'leasing'. However, it can also include asset-based loans, where there is no bailment, as the borrower owns the asset. Most asset finance agreements, however, are leases as asset-based loans remain relatively uncommon.

HISTORY

Early development

The bailment of assets can be traced back to Babylonian law, with many of the legal principles in place today heavily influenced by Roman law.

Leasing, as a means of acquiring business capital assets, first developed significantly in the nineteenth century railway industry. One of the earliest leasing companies was the Birmingham Wagon Company, formed in 1854 to lease wagons to colliery owners. The North Central Wagon Company of Rotherham was founded in 1861, and still exists in the form of Lombard, part of NatWest.

Between the two world wars leasing was used by some machinery suppliers to restrict access to their new types of manufacturing equipment to customers willing to sign long-term lease commitments. In the UK the leasing industry then developed only slowly until the 1960s.

1960s

At this time some major specialist leasing companies set up in the UK, including the Mercantile Leasing Company, a joint venture of the United States Leasing Company and the Mercantile Credit Company.

Existing providers of hire purchase in the consumer credit market and some of the merchant banks also established companies for the leasing of industrial equipment.

The industry grew strongly in the late 1960s as IBM, and later other computer companies, began to offer leasing options to their customers.

Lessors became eligible to claim investment grants on leased assets from 1966. Restrictions on the amount of credit that could be provided to non-bank leasing companies placed such companies at a disadvantage to bank and foreign lessors.

By the end of the 1960s around £100 million per year of new asset finance i.e. leasing and hire purchase provided to businesses was being arranged (£1.5bn today).

1970s

Following the introduction of tax capital allowances in 1970, the Government introduced 100 percent first year tax capital allowances in 1972. Leasing also became eligible for other forms of Government support intended to promote business investment. This all led to the steady expansion of the finance lease industry.

Leasing subsidiaries of clearing banks including Barclays, Williams & Glyn's and the Royal Bank of Scotland were set up to utilise the capital allowances, which were particularly valuable to the banks who were paying 52 percent tax on their profits.

The Consumer Credit Act 1974 replaced and expanded previous restrictions on, and regulation of the hire purchase industry. It extended regulation to hire and credit agreements provided to unincorporated businesses for values under £15,000.

By the end of the 1970s around £1.2 billion per year of new asset finance was being arranged (£6.2bn today).

1980s

The 1984 Finance Act scaled down capital allowances, with a maximum allowance of 25 percent per year on a reducing balance basis for most assets.

Also in 1984 a new accounting standard for leases, SSAP 21, resulted in lessees being required to report many leased assets on their own balance sheets for the first time.

By the end of the 1980s around £12.0 billion per year of new asset finance was being arranged (£31bn today).

1990s

Several large banks sold off their leasing operations. G.E. Capital Corporation acquired part of Mercantile Credit in July 1991 from Barclays.

The UK recession of 1990-91 led to a fall in the market of around 10% with a return to normal levels by 1995. By the end of the 1990s around £18 billion per year of new asset finance was being arranged (£33bn today).

2000s

The decade was marked by a dramatic fall of more than 30% in new business between 2008 (£27bn) and 2009 (£18.4bn) following the 2008 crisis in the global financial markets. Non-banks were particularly badly hit as some were unable to access any funding, nor the very low cost funds available through the Bank of England to the large banks.

There was a gradual erosion of tax benefits of finance leases due to a combination of the long-funding lease rules, lower corporation tax rates and lower interest rates. This contributed to a decline in big-ticket leasing written in the UK.

2010s

From 2010 there was a slow but steady recovery in the market, with volumes and market shares back to pre-global financial crisis levels by 2016. This was followed by several years of strong growth, reflecting overall UK business investment.

The industry became more diverse with the share of the market taken by firms other than UK banks also growing to over 50% for the first time, and over 50% of funding being from firms owned outside of the UK. By 2019, annual new business was £35.7bn (£44bn today).

2020s

The start of the decade was marked by the COVID-19 recession, with an unprecedented drop in economic activity during the first national lockdown in 2020. Following the restrictions put in place for the crisis, Asset finance new business fell by 49% in the second quarter of 2020 compared to the same period in 2019. However, it then recovered somewhat in the second half of 2020, ending the year down by 23%. The market then grew by 14% in 2021 and a further 6% in 2022, returning to pre-Covid levels in 2023.

Following the 2016 referendum, the UK left the European Union in 2020, with no obvious immediate impact on the leasing industry as all European-owned lessors continued to invest in the UK market.

The FLA reported total new lending in 2023 of £38.3bn.

A-Z OF TERMS

A

Acceptance certificate

A confirmation signed by the lessee that the assets to be leased have been received complete, in full, in good condition, and are fit for use. Upon receipt by the lessor of such signed confirmation from the lessee, the lease agreement will usually start.

Use of an acceptance certificate procedure may delay the start of the lease, but it is a sensible 'stop and check' which can benefit both lessee and lessor. The lessee's risk of being committed to lease payments for assets, which are not yet delivered, not as required or faulty, is reduced. The lessor is less likely to pay a fraudulent supplier or to have to deal with a complaint or default. UK Courts are unlikely to pay heed to such a certificate if it was signed by the customer prior to actual delivery of the assets.

An equivalent (or sometimes additional) confirmation may be obtained by phone rather than in writing. Some lessors use a 'deemed acceptance' clause in the lease agreement to place the onus on the lessee to inform them of any problems with the assets delivered.

Deemed acceptance clauses will usually have a time limit starting at the date of delivery. This means that the lessee will have a set number of days from the date of delivery of the asset to inform the lessor of any problems or the lessee will be deemed to have accepted the asset, triggering the start of the lease agreement.

#Legal #Risk

Acceptance ratio

The proportion of total applications that are accepted following underwriting. Funders will wish to keep the acceptance ratio high and avoid unnecessary underwriting expense, by providing clear guidance on their lending policies to their direct salesforce and introducers.

It can also be useful to monitor acceptance ratio by introducer, where appropriate. This can help to identify where action is needed either to reduce the level of unacceptable proposals or to review the underwriting policy.

#Credit

Accelerated depreciation

Any method of accounting depreciation that results in a comparatively large expense in the early years of an asset's life and a lower expense in the later years. As a largely historical example, the Sum of the digits approach, also known as Rule of 78, was commonly used until replaced by the Actuarial method. Compared to a constant level of depreciation, an accelerated approach can lead to lower reported profits in the earlier years of a lease and higher in the later years.

#Accounting

Accounting standards

The rules and guidance for financial reporting that all companies are required to follow when preparing their accounts to be filed at Companies House.

Lease accounting rules in the UK are now contained in Financial Reporting Standards (FRS) issued by the Financial Reporting Council. The FRSs include the core Standard, FRS 102, the simplified FRS 105 for micro-entities (e.g. many companies with turnover below £632,000), and FRS 101 which provides for reduced disclosures for certain subsidiary and other companies. Previously there was a separate standard for leases, Statement of Standard Accounting Practice (SSAP) 21.

Listed companies, banks and insurance companies must follow international accounting standards issued by the International Accounting Standards Board for their consolidated accounts. International Financial Reporting Standard 16 (IFRS

16) replaced International Accounting Standard 17 for reporting leases in periods ending from January 2019.

IFRS 16 rules for lease accounting are due to be extended to UK FRS standards for reporting from 2026.

#Accounting

Actuarial method

A method of calculating finance lease interest income for lessor accounting. It is based on the principle that a lessor will earn a constant return on its investment in each period of the lease agreement. The effective interest rate of the lease is therefore used to calculate the interest component of each lease payment. As the lessee repays the principal, the interest earned therefore reduces.

It is considered a more precise way of calculating income than the simpler Rule of 78. Auditors would expect the actuarial method to be used unless the difference between the two methods is found not to be material.

Whichever method is used (Actuarial, or Rule of 78) the interest income reported by lessors in their financial accounts will be different to the cash received. This is partly because only the interest is reported as income and not the repayment of the principal, and partly because the timing of the income recognition is based on one of these two theoretical approaches.

The Actuarial rate of return is the percentage margin between the interest income calculated using the actuarial method and the lessor's own cost of finance.

#Accounting

Additions

Often refers to extra features added to leased assets by the lessee. The lease agreement will typically require the lessor to agree to any such modifications, and the additions will become part of the property of the lessor. It will also typically include an obligation for the lessee to insure such additions.

The term is also used to refer to lessees adding additional assets to an existing Master lease agreement, for example adding extra cars to an existing fleet. That will typically be documented by the lessor and lessee entering into an equipment schedule to the Master lease agreement.

#Contracts

Administration

When a trading entity in financial difficulty enters administration, a court can make an Administration Order to appoint an Insolvency Practitioner (the 'IP'). The Order allows for the reorganisation of a company or for it or its assets to be sold. During the administration, which usually lasts for up to 12 months, there is a moratorium on the company's debts.

The IP will establish the likelihood of the company being able to trade its way out of difficulty. The IP has powers to make decisions to effect change within the business and its current structure. They take over the responsibilities of the company's directors and draw remuneration from the company's trading receipts.

The administrator must act in the best interests of all creditors, including lessors. Difficulties can arise if the IP is not able to establish if some assets are leased where the IP is slow to inform and consult with a lessor, or where the IP does not ensure that the leased assets remain insured and maintained.

#Legal #Risk

Advance

The amount paid out by the lessor to the supplier of the Assets once a lease agreement commences. It is usually paid after an Acceptance certificate is obtained. The advance paid by the lessor is subject to VAT, which the lessor will usually recover from HMRC.

#Contracts

Advance lease payments

Where the lessee is required to make one or more lease payments in advance of the start of the lease. Such payments may take the form either of a payment in advance (e.g. the first month's rental paid at the inception of the lease), or a security deposit that will then reduce the last payment or payments of the lease. Advance lease payments provide added security to the lessor by reducing their initial exposure.

Advance lease payments are usually separate from any deposit that the lessee may pay to the lessor or the supplier of assets that reduces the amount under the lease agreement.

#Contracts

Advanced Internal Ratings Based Approach (AIRB)

For prudential regulation, the optional method by which banks can calculate their Risk Weighted Assets (RWA). It is an alternative to the Standardised Approach. AIRB risk weightings are an output of risk models developed by banks and approved by the Prudential Regulation Authority. They allow banks to estimate their Loss Given Defaults, rather than using standards set by the regulations.

The AIRB is relatively expensive to set up and run, as it requires large volumes of data. It has the potential to recognise the relatively low risk nature of leasing, which can help banks to offer the most competitive rates for leases (the lower the RWA, the lower the cost of lending). Some banks using AIRB bundle all SME loans together and although the risk weighting will then usually be preferable to that used by banks using the Standardised Approach, it will not recognise the low risk nature of leasing.

The competitive advantage that can be gained by the largest banks has long been a concern for their smaller competitors. The Prudential Regulation Authority has responded by allowing banks without extensive historical data on loan defaults to supplement their own internal data with external (pooled) market data in calculating credit risk weighted assets. That might assist smaller or less established banks for some types of lending, but not in leasing where there is no comprehensive sharing of information on default experience.

New international prudential rules from the Basel Committee, Basel 3.1, set an 'output floor' (or lower limit) to RWA calculations using the AIRB. The floor is, broadly, 72.5% of RWA calculated using the Standardised Approach as it applies to credit. In the

UK, the final rules implementing Basel 3.1, were expected to be completed during 2024, with implementation over the period from 2025 to 2030. The new floor will limit the advantages obtained by banks using the AIRB.

#Prudential

Advantages of leasing

The benefits of leasing vary dependent upon the type of lease and the lessee's circumstances but will include some combination of the following:

Lower cost than using retained earnings or unsecured bank loans to pay for assets due to:

- Lower risk of default (see Probability of Default) on leases compared to bank loans
- Lower losses for defaulted agreements (see Loss Given Default) on leases compared to bank loans
- Lessee may be eligible to claim tax relief on part or all the lease payments
- Lessor may be eligible for tax capital allowances when the lessee may not have tax capacity
- The lessor may be able to dispose of assets at lower cost or for higher value
- Availability of 'zero percent' or other 'subsidised' finance from manufacturers.

Easier to obtain than bank loans:

- Additional source of finance for a business that has limited cash and constrained access to bank loans
- Less need to provide additional security, including liens over business or directors' personal assets
- Less need to review or renegotiate covenants in existing loans or securities.

Reduces risks compared to using retained earnings or bank loans to pay for assets:

- Asset finance cannot be withdrawn during the term of an agreement
- Lessee may avoid residual value risk on leased assets
- Lessee will avoid interest rate risk if lease payments are fixed not variable.

Provides additional benefits:

- Helps firms to manage cashflow better, as lease costs can be broadly aligned with expected income arising from the firm's use of the asset
- Agreement may provide for a replacement to be provided if leased asset requires maintenance or repair
- Special deals for upgrades to newer technology may be available to lessees using captive finance companies or manufacturer-supported vendor finance schemes.

#Alternatives

Affordability

For the FCA's regulation of consumer credit, lessors must specifically assess whether a regulated consumer or business customer will be able to pay for a new lease.

Lessors might consider a range of factors in making their assessment including whether the new agreement will replace an existing lease that the lessee has paid without problems; the size of the agreement relative to the size of the business; a credit agency's report on the business; and a review of the lessee's business, financial position and its plans.

The FCA has made clear that a credit check based on historic information is insufficient and it is also necessary to consider the potential for new loans to become unaffordable.

Regulated firms should keep records of the basis of their assessments of affordability. The FCA states that it expects affordability procedures to be 'reasonable' and 'appropriate in the particular circumstances', which might suggest a relatively high-level approach for business customers, but it is still important that suitable affordability policies and procedures are in place and can be shown to have been followed.

#Conduct

Agency agreement

The contract used where a supplier or manufacturer of assets (the 'agent') enters lease agreements with its customers on behalf of and in accordance with the instructions of a lessor (the 'principal').

The agency arrangement may be disclosed or undisclosed. If the agreement is disclosed, the lessee will be informed that the agent is acting on behalf of a particular principal. In these scenarios, the lessor will often collect the lease payments from the lessee.

Alternatively, if the agency arrangement is undisclosed, the lessee will not know of the existence of the principal under the agency arrangement. In these scenarios, the agent will collect the lease payments on behalf of the principal and remit those payments to the principal.

There are other types of agency arrangements in law, whereby an intermediary agent is involved in contractual dealings between a principal and the principal's customer (see for instance Agency purchase below). However, within leasing, the arrangement described above is one of the most common and significant ones.

#Contracts

Agency purchase

The agency arrangement whereby a lessee is authorised by the lessor to acquire assets on its behalf. In this way the lessee may order assets from a supplier on the basis that the supplier will invoice the lessor on delivery. It can form part of a wider pre-lease agreement with the supplier.

#Legal

A Agent

For the FCA's regulation of consumer credit, an individual who is appointed by a firm to act as its representative in dealing with customers.

The agent can only work for one firm (the 'principal' firm) and must make clear that they are representing that firm. For the customer it should make no difference whether the firm's representative is an employee or an agent. The agent does not need their own FCA authorisation as the principal accepts responsibility for the agent's conduct. The principal must ensure its agents are properly supervised with a suitable agreement in place but does not need to register individual agents with the FCA.

Some asset finance brokers appoint agents. For a smaller broker, there may be only one or two agents who are semi-retired or working part-time. Some larger brokers may appoint multiple agents to help build their geographical coverage.

In law, the term refers more generally to any person appointed to represent the interests of another party (the principal). Various legal cases in recent years have considered whether finance brokers are acting as agents of either the lender or the borrower, and the implications for their obligations, including what information they should provide on commissions. Brokers have duties as agents on both sides of the introductions they are making, with the extent of the duties resting largely on how the broker describes their role, and their agreements with lenders.

#Conduct #Intermediaries

Aircraft leasing

The largest part of the global equipment leasing market by value, lessors own around one-third of the global aircraft fleet. According to the Centre for Aviation Fleet Database in the USA, 53% of commercial aircraft globally are leased. This is 20,000 of the total of 38,000 commercial aircraft. Lessors' share of orders is much lower, around 23%, because many aircraft are purchased by the airline and then refinanced using Sale and Leaseback arrangements.

The largest lessors include Aercap with 1,700 owned aircraft, Avolon with 1,000 aircraft, and SMBC Aviation Capital (formerly RBS Aviation Capital) with 700 aircraft.

The sector comes with its own distinct terminology. In a dry lease the lessee operates the aircraft. In a wet lease they are operated by the lessor who is an airline itself. A damp (sometimes called 'moist') lease is a wet lease that comes without the cabin crew.

Dublin is a major global centre for the aviation leasing industry, partly because of Ireland's low rate of corporation tax but increasingly reflecting the expertise in place there. Over 60% of the world's leased aircraft, with an estimated value of more than $100 billion, are managed from Ireland, according to Aircraft Leasing Ireland (ALI), the group representing the aircraft leasing industry in Ireland

#Market

Alternative finance

Finance that is 'non-conventional' as it is provided from outside of the banking system. It includes crowdfunding, peer-to-peer lending, and invoice trading where businesses sell their invoices through an online marketplace. Leasing is too well-established to be classified by most people as alternative finance, although the leasing market is probably the largest provider of non-bank business debt finance.

#Alternatives

Amortisation

For lease accounting, an accounting estimate of the reduction in the value of a lease as lease payments are made over time. A lease is said to be fully amortised once the whole of the original capital value less any residual value has been repaid with interest. It is calculated using the Effective interest method.

The amortised cost is the amount at which the lessor values the lease. It comprises the initial amount recognised, minus the cumulative amortisation, adjusted for any loss allowance.

#Accounting

A Annual Investment Allowance (AIA)

Capital Allowances tax rules that allow companies to deduct the full value of a qualifying asset from their profit before tax in the year they buy it.

AIA rules allow businesses to deduct up to £1 million per year. Successive governments and chancellors have altered the limit regularly, but the £1 million rate was announced as 'permanent' in 2023. In addition, from 2023 to 2026 a 'full expensing' scheme allows unlimited 100% capital allowances for qualifying new investments.

AIAs only bring forward capital allowances from later years, they do not increase the overall tax deductions available when investing in assets.

Many leases qualify for the AIA, including hire purchase and long funding leases, but operating leases and finance leases with no transfer of ownership do not qualify. Interest on a hire purchase is a trading expense, so capital allowances do not apply to that part of the total cost.

In the former Government's Autumn Budget Statement in 2023, it committed to working with the leasing industry 'with a view to identifying a solution that supports the leasing sector to access the benefits of full expensing whilst managing the risks of abuse and error.' A joint HM Treasury and HMRC Capital Allowances and Leasing working group was established, with the ambition being for the Government to 'publish draft legislation on this issue for consultation in due course'. This appears to be looking at ways of extending AIAs to types of leasing that do not already qualify. It is unclear whether the new Labour Government will progress the plans.

Lessees eligible to claim capital allowances, including for hire purchase agreements, can benefit from the AIA if they have sufficient taxable profits to offset. AIAs are not available for cars unless they are fully electric.

#Tax

Annualised Percentage Rate (APR)

The annual rate of interest on a credit agreement. For regulated consumer credit, the APR exists to allow customers to compare offerings and is calculated in a standard way to include all costs which the borrower will pay under the terms of the agreement. These include interest, fees and any other charges, whether payable to the lender or to anyone else. The APR is the rate at which the amount of credit advanced is equal to the sum of the present values of each repayment of capital and of each payment in respect of the total charge for credit.

There are complex rules in the CCA and relevant Regulations on how APRs may be used in marketing. For example, advertisements that feature interest rates must show a 'Representative APR', which will be the APR at or below which the advertiser reasonably expects, at the date on which the credit advertisement is published, that credit would be provided under at least 51% of the consumer credit agreements which will be entered into as a result of the advertisement.

#Conduct #Legal

Annual service fee

Some lessors charge lessees an annual fee in addition to their regular lease payments. Those charging the fee tend to point to the on-going costs of monitoring the contract and asset risk, rather than the increased cost of overall credit.

For agreements regulated by the CCA, this fee should be included in the Annualised Percentage Rate calculation. Under the FCA consumer duty rules, like other parts of the price, the fees should represent fair value.

#Contracts

Anti-Money Laundering (AML)

Steps to prevent the financial system being used to facilitate crime and terrorism. Lessors and their brokers and introducers need to check they are dealing with representatives of genuine businesses.

Some factors indicate that leasing is a relatively low risk activity for money laundering. Funds are not released to the lessee but rather to the supplier of the assets, payments are usually collected from pre-existing UK bank accounts of the lessees by direct debit and cash payments are not normally accepted.

On the other hand, leasing could be a low-cost way of obtaining assets to be used in criminal or terrorist activities. Early settlement of agreements could also potentially be a way of distributing illegally obtained money.

Both the FCA and the Joint Money Laundering Steering Group publish guidance on AML checks. All lessors (other than sole traders) need to register with an AML supervisor, usually the FCA, and should have a designated Money Laundering Reporting Officer (MLRO).

From 2024, lessors whose UK revenue exceeds £10.2 million per year are required to pay the Economic Crime Levy.

#Regulation

Appointed Representative (AR)

For FCA consumer credit regulation, a firm or individual who carries out regulated activities on behalf of a firm that is directly authorised by the FCA (the 'principal' firm). The AR is not then directly authorised by the FCA.

The AR must inform a regulated customer that it is acting as an AR of the principal firm, but it can trade under a different name. The principal must have a written agreement with the AR, must register the AR with the FCA and is responsible for making sure that the AR is fit and proper and complies with the rules of the FCA.

A variant of AR is Introducer Appointed Representative ('IAR'). An IAR is a non-FCA authorised firm that has been appointed by an FCA authorised firm to perform limited regulated activity, namely, to introduce a regulated customer to the principal firm or other members of that firm's group. An IAR cannot discuss or otherwise get involved in the customer's financial needs. The IAR is therefore generally seen as less risky for the principal than an AR.

Some asset finance brokers appoint other smaller brokers as their ARs and dealers as either ARs or IARs. Few lessors have chosen to take on the responsibility for supervising other firms in this way.

#Conduct #Intermediaries

Appraisal

An expert report on the current and expected future value of an asset, likely to be based on an inspection and knowledge of the second-hand market. It is generally used by lessors for higher value assets. Due to the cost, lessors tend to rely on their own checks and asset expertise, or that of trusted specialist brokers, for most types of equipment. May also be called valuation.

#Assets

Appropriation of funds

For regulated agreements, if the customer is in arrears on more than one contract and a payment is received, the lessor must decide how to appropriate, or direct, the funds to the different contracts. Under FCA rules, the customer should be permitted to decide how to split the payment. If the customer does not do so, the payment should be split proportionally between the agreements (i.e. the account with the largest balance attracts the highest payment).

#Conduct

Arena Television

The biggest fraud to hit the UK asset finance industry, Arena Television was one of the UK's largest outdoor broadcasting companies, facilitating coverage of football, racing and music events including the Glastonbury festival.

The business went into administration in 2021, owing an estimated £285m to 55 different asset finance providers, and leading to a criminal investigation of the directors by the UK's Serious Fraud Office.

The directors were alleged to have falsified serial numbers for assets to facilitate multiple financing fraud. Of the 55 lenders caught up in the fraud, there were no assets to support lending by 46 firms. One reason the fraud could be perpetuated was Arena TV's ability to convince some finance companies that routine asset inspections, a normal due diligence step, could not be completed because the assets concerned were supposedly being used on-site at events.

The incident led to the establishment of a new database of asset finance lending, namely 'Lumia' operated by Acquis Data Services.

The Prudential Regulation Authority conducted a review of key themes and control weaknesses that the case identified. In its report in November 2022, it noted that 'The large number of UK lenders with connections to the failed Arena Holdings Group, and the total exposure across all the lenders being disproportionate to the size of Arena.

Arena, raised questions around the robustness of banks' credit risk management frameworks and controls in the asset finance sector'. The key control weaknesses identified were:

- Risk appetite in relation to Single Name Concentration (i.e. single lessee) risk
- Inadequate levels of inspection and verification of assets
- Weaknesses in vetting of equipment suppliers
- Lack of an industry asset register

#Risk

Arrears

Money owed by the lessee to the lessor that should already have been paid. Arrears may be caused by a failed direct debit payment due to lack of funds or a payment stopped by the customer. There might also be technical errors in setting up or amending direct debit arrangements.

Average arrears levels across the industry are typically between 1% and 2% of the value of lessors' books. Leaseurope research shows that most leasing arrears cases are resolved, so do not proceed to become defaults.

Separately, the term can instead simply refer to an option for how lease payments are made. That is, instead of payment being required 'in advance' at the beginning of each period, it may be due 'in arrears' at the end of each period.

#Credit

Artificial Intelligence (AI)

The use of software algorithms that are learning how to solve problems previously only associated with human decision-making. The predicted impacts of AI are so great that it is often called the 'Fourth Industrial Revolution' and AI is now being used in many applications in financial services.

Here are some areas where AI might be relevant in asset finance include:

- Combining and using multiple sources of data to predict credit risk of new lending and the existing book.
- Analysing transaction data alongside other information to highlight potentially fraudulent transactions.
- Lessees extracting key information from large numbers of lease contracts for the preparation of accounting information.
- Automation of routine operations, such as capturing information from invoices and other paperwork.

#Operations

Asset

Any items of plant, property and equipment that might be leased. In general, items termed 'plant' are regarded as immovable whereas items termed 'equipment' are generally movable. In addition to these tangible items, some intangible assets such as software licences might also be leased. Assets may also be categorised as Hard assets or Soft assets for leasing purposes.

#Assets

Asset-Backed Commercial Paper (ABCP)

Short-term debt securities backed by assets from multiple sellers that may include asset finance portfolios. ABCP is issued by a conduit, or structured investment vehicle, usually set up by a sponsoring bank. ABCP is used by lessors in the United States and Canada but lessors in Europe generally issue Asset-Backed Securities.

#Funding

Asset-Backed Securities (ABS)

Debt securities that may be issued by lessors, most commonly by captive car lessors.

The lessor's payments to the investors in the debt are backed by rights to portfolios of lease agreements and the assets underlying those agreements. The portfolio of leases may be placed in a special purpose vehicle (SPV). In the event of the lessor not being able to pay the investors, the income from the leases would then be paid directly from the SPV to the investors.

Some ABS issued by lessors in Europe is raised without the use of an SPV. This approach helps to manage the debt issuance costs. The investors would still have rights to a portfolio of leases that can change over time. The security of the assets is supported by guarantees from a captive's parent company, or a bank or another sponsor. Many European asset finance issues have also been supported by the European Investment Fund.

#Funding

Asset based finance

Business lending secured against invoices issued by the business but not yet paid. Lending secured against invoices is termed factoring if it includes debt management and collection services, or invoice discounting if not.

#Alternatives

Asset Based Lending (ABL)

Business lending where assets are used as collateral for loans. Unlike leasing, the lender does not own the assets but instead has security rights over them. Examples include aviation mortgages and marine mortgages.

ABL tends to be used for higher value assets, as the costs of setting up the security arrangements can be high, and the process for the lender to recover an asset following a default can be more complicated compared to leasing. The method can help to reduce the lender's exposure, whether it is reputational or wider, to risk associated with possible incidents when the asset it used.

#Alternatives

Asset disposal

The process by which lessors deal with equipment that is returned to them at end of lease. It may be sold, leased to a different customer, recycled, or scrapped.

The lease agreement might specify that the lessee will dispose of it on behalf of the lessor. In that case the lessee might be entitled to keep most of the proceeds of the sale. This can provide an extra incentive for the lessee to keep the asset in good condition.

The lessor might have an arrangement with a broker or equipment supplier to sell or take back the equipment (see Remarketing agreement, Repurchase agreement). If equipment does come back to the lessor, it can be sold, offered on a lease to a new customer, disposed of for scrap or recycled.

Lessors can have responsibilities under data protection law to ensure that any confidential data has been removed from relevant asset types. The Asset Disposal and Information Security Alliance issues guidance on good practice in meeting this responsibility.

What might once have been seen as a relatively unimportant part of the leasing value chain is now becoming a key point of competitive advantage and differentiation. As part of the trend towards the 'circular economy' lessees increasingly want to know that their returned equipment will be dealt with in the most environmentally friendly way possible.

#Assets

Asset finance

Usually refers to any business credit or hire arrangements where the lender or hirer owns the equipment during the period of the credit or hire period. Includes finance lease, operating lease, hire purchase, contract hire and other products. Virtually synonymous with the term 'leasing' except that leasing would also cover property. A hire agreement of up to one year would generally be considered a rental product and not asset finance.

It may also be defined wider to include Instalment Credit loans that are arranged specifically to allow the borrower to acquire an asset. While the legal ownership of the asset transfers to the borrower at the start of the contract, the terms and conditions allow for the asset to be recovered by the lender if the terms are not met.

#Market

Asset Finance 50

Annual ranking survey of UK lessors, first published in 2016 by Asset Finance Policy and Asset Finance International. The tables show lessors' net investment in business equipment leasing based on their published accounts.

In 2024, the top 50 firms showed total net investment in UK leasing of £44.5 billion. This includes the net present value of finance lease receivables, excluding impairments and unearned interest, plus the undiscounted value of minimum operating lease receivables.

The top ten firms accounted for around 60% of the market. 50% of the total outstandings were issued by UK-owned lessors, 28% by European banks, and 22% by internationally owned firms. Banks accounted for 70% of the market.

The largest firms are shown at the back of this book and the full survey is available to download from the Asset Finance Connect website. *www.assetfinanceconnect.com*

#Market

Asset Finance Connect

Digital and in-person events for auto, equipment, and asset finance communities. Holds regular conferences in the UK and Europe, an annual industry awards event, and interactive online events.

Free-to-access website which provides news, analysis, and editorial commentary on industry issues.

Co-publishers with Asset Finance Policy of the Asset Finance 50 and Asset Finance Europe 50, the annual ranking surveys of the UK and Europe's largest asset finance providers respectively.
www.assetfinanceconnect.com

#Market

Asset Finance Professionals Association (AF-PA)

A forum for professionals from the asset finance industry to network informally and to raise funds for member nominated charities. It holds bi-annual receptions in London and various other events. Through its wider network, it also aims to help anyone in the industry to realise their personal and professional goals and seeks to promote the highest professional standards.
www.af-pa.org

#Associations

Asset refinance

An alternative term for Sale and leaseback.

#Products

Asset register

To help prevent theft, fraud including double financing, and to help protect assets if a lessee becomes insolvent or enters administration, lessors may wish to record their ownership of assets on a publicly available register.

Any on-road vehicle has a Vehicle Identification Number (VIN) and lessors will register their financial interest against this on a database operated by HPI Limited, a subsidiary of the American company Solera Holdings.

Other assets may also be registered on HPI using serial numbers. Unlike with VINs the HPI system cannot verify the serial number against the type of asset. Accuracy in recording and checking numbers is therefore essential.

For many years the legal profession has been exploring ways in which lessors and others could register their interest in assets at Companies House, but this has not yet proven feasible other than in Scotland, where under the Moveable Transactions (Scotland) Act 2023 a Register of Assignations was due to be set up in 2024. The new Register in Scotland deals with a particular feature of Scottish law around the treatment of sale and hire purchase back arrangements, rather than general leasing arrangements.

Following the Arena Television fraud case, a new exposure register, Lumia, was established in 2023.

Serial number labels on assets can be altered or replaced by fraudsters. The Construction & Agricultural Equipment Security and Registration Scheme (CESAR) is designed to overcome this problem for plant and machinery.

#Assets #Risk

Assignment

The transfer of legal rights from one person (the 'assignor') to another (the 'assignee').

A lessee might transfer its rights to use the asset, or a lessor might transfer its rights to receive rentals for the remaining lease term. Technically, at law, only the 'benefit' of a contract can be assigned (i.e. the lessee's right to use an asset or the lessor's right to receive rentals). The 'burden' of a contract cannot be assigned (i.e. the lessee's obligation to pay rentals or the lessor's general obligations under the contract). This means that the assignor will remain liable to perform the burden of the contract event after the assignment has taken place. To transfer the rights and burden of a contract, see Novation.

Lease agreements will typically require the lessee to obtain the lessor's consent if the lessee wishes to assign such lease agreement. That is because, apart from keeping good records, the lessor will be concerned that the assignment could increase the risk of default if the assignee (i.e. the new lessee) has a lower credit rating compared to the original lessee.

Assignments can either be disclosed or undisclosed. This will be determined by whether a notice of assignment has been served on the other party to the contract (that is, if notice has been served, the assignment will be disclosed, and if notice has not been served, the assignment will be undisclosed). Disclosure is important as it may determine what type of assignment it is. 'Legal assignments' allow the assignee to enforce the assigned rights themselves without the need to include the assignor. 'Equitable assignments' require the assignee to either rely on the assignor to enforce the assigned rights or bring action together with the assignor. One of the requirements for a legal assignment is disclosure/notice of assignment.

There may, however, exist compelling reasons not to disclose the assignment and to have only an equitable assignment. Choosing to do so will, however, carry an increased risk to the assignee as they will need to rely on the assignor.

If there are valid reasons for a lease to be transferred away from a lessee, for example the lessee is acquired, the lessor will normally prefer to novate the lease to the new party (see Novation). This is because it avoids the potential technical complications set out in this section.

Other reasons why a lessor may want to transfer lease agreements include situations where a lessor's book is in run-off, or if a lessor places a portfolio of leases in a special purpose vehicle as part of a securitisation.

#Legal

Aviation mortgage

Asset based lending secured by an aircraft. It is an example of asset-based finance and an example of a Chattel mortgage.

#Products

Audit

The formal inspection of accounts by a qualified external accountant. As part of the audit report, the auditor is legally obliged, under Companies Act 2006, to provide an opinion on whether the accounts give a true and fair view of the company's affairs.

Most UK companies are now exempt from the need to have their accounts audited. Exemptions apply to companies with at least two of the following: An annual turnover of no more than £10.2 million. assets worth no more than £5.1 million, and fifty or fewer employees on average

Even without an audit statement, the involvement of an external professional accountant, usually a member of one of the chartered accountancy bodies registered as a 'member in practice', may still provide a degree of assurance to underwriters over the accuracy of the accounts, but the scope of the work carried out can vary significantly.

#Accounting #Credit

B

Back to back lease

Where assets are leased to a lessee and that lessee subsequently sub-leases those assets to a sub-lessee on the same terms. See also Head lessor.

#Contracts

Bad debt

Amounts owed to a lessor that are no longer expected to be paid. They are written-off as losses for accounting purposes. A more common term used in the industry is defaulted.

#Credit #Risk

Bailment

Broadly, the temporary transfer of possession (and not ownership) of goods by the owner (the bailor) to another person (the bailee) so that they might be used for a specified purpose on condition that they are returned to, or in accordance with the instructions of, the bailor, or kept until he reclaims them. The bailee does not own the goods but has possession of them.

Under the Supply of Goods and Services Act 1982 the lessor cannot disturb the lessee's 'quiet possession' of the leased asset provided the terms of the agreement are being met.

#Legal

Balance financed

The price paid for the assets less any deposit paid by the customer direct to the supplier.

#Contract

Balance sheet

Financial statement showing the financial position of a business at a specific point in time. The statement will show the firm's assets, liabilities, and shareholders' funds. Under UK accounting rules until 2026, the lessee's balance sheet will include assets leased using finance leases but not operating leases. Under IFRS 16 and UK accounting rules from 2026, it includes all leased assets.

#Accounting

Balloon payment

A final payment for an asset finance agreement that is larger than the previous monthly or other periodic payments. Often referred to simply as a balloon. It is most commonly found on hire purchase contracts, for which ownership of the asset will transfer to the lessee only after payment of the balloon (provided the lessee has paid all the instalments and all such other sums that may be due under the finance agreement). The size of the balloon is set when the lease is entered into and is not linked to the residual value of the asset.

Lessees need to understand their obligation to pay the balloon. When comparing lease options, lessees also need to consider the overall cost of the lease, not only the regular payments.

#Contracts

Bank lessor

A deposit-taking bank that is a lessor itself or a leasing subsidiary of a bank. Seven of the largest UK lessors are banks. The largest bank lessors, according to the Asset Finance 50, are Royal Bank of Scotland (including its subsidiary, Lombard), HSBC, Lloyds, Santander, Close and Aldermore.

#Market

Bank of England

The UK's Central Bank. The Prudential Regulation Authority (PRA) is part of the Bank. The BoE conducts market operations in which it buys aims to boost lending in the economy.
www.bankofengland.co.uk

#Bodies

Bank of International Settlements (BIS)

The body that facilitates collaboration between national central banks.

Established in 1930 and based in Basel, Switzerland, the BIS has sixty central bank members from around the world. Its mission is to serve central banks in their pursuit of monetary and financial stability, to foster international cooperation in those areas and to function as a bank for central banks.

The BIS's Basel Committee on Banking Supervision sets standards for the Prudential regulation and supervision of banks which are then implemented by the Bank of England in the UK and the European Central Bank for the Eurozone. Although individual central banks have some flexibility in

implementation, the prudential treatment of leasing rests largely on the Committee's work.
www.bis.org

#Bodies #Prudential

Bank Referral Scheme

Under the Bank Referral Scheme, large UK banks are obliged to offer small businesses whose applications for finance leases (and other types of loans) are rejected a referral to a designated online platform that may be able to help find alternative sources of finance. The alternative platforms available each include asset finance funders. The Scheme is overseen by the British Business Bank and was launched in 2016. It is intended to address the 'funding gap' caused by declined applications for finance.

#Regulation

Bankruptcy

The process by which an individual, who may or may not be in business, is declared bankrupt by a Court. The individual's assets, with certain exceptions, are converted into money and distributed among their creditors to satisfy debt. Creditors are unable to pursue parties that have been made bankrupt. See also Insolvency.

#Legal #Risk

Bargain purchase option

The opportunity for the lessee to purchase a leased asset at the end of the lease term at a price that is significantly below the asset's fair market value.

Given the low price, many lessees can be expected to take up the option. Many hire purchase agreements include bargain purchase options, also commonly called option to purchase. For tax purposes only those agreements that have bargain purchase options are classified as hire purchase agreements.

#Contracts

Bargain renewal option

The opportunity for the lessee to extend the lease at the end of the lease term at a rate significantly below the normal market level. This could be a Peppercorn rate. Given the low cost many lessees can be expected to take up the option. The term is used for lease accounting and is not otherwise in common use.

#Accounting #Contracts

Basel Committee

See Bank of International Settlements.

#Bodies #Prudential

Basis point

An interest rate difference of one-hundredth of a percentage point.

#Finance

Battery-as-a-Service (BaaS)

Providing batteries, typically for electric cars, on a rental or lease arrangement. The term was originally used to describe 'battery swapping' whereby a driver might be able to exchange a battery during a long journey, although that has not proven to be practicable. It now refers instead to providing a longer-term battery lease, arranged through a separate contract to the electric vehicle lease.

Although take-up remains low at present, there are forecasts of growth in demand for BaaS to deal with concerns about battery degradation in electric vehicles. In theory the battery could be leased from a different provider to the vehicle.

#ESG

BEN

The Motor and Allied Trades Benevolent Fund, a not-for-profit organisation, dedicated to those who work, or have worked, in the automotive industry and their family dependents. BEN offers practical help, support and advice, and it operates highly-regarded care centres. It is supported by many organisations in the vehicle leasing market.

#Market

Big-ticket lease

Leasing of high-value assets such as aircraft, ships, and trains. The FLA refers to 'high value' leases which are for projects over £20 million, the ELFA to financings over $5 million. Such agreements typically involve specialist legal and tax expertise.

Big-ticket leasing in the UK has declined greatly with the demise of major tax incentives. In 2002 it represented 25% of new leasing by value and in 2023 it was 5%, despite the £20 million threshold having fallen by nearly half in real terms. Big ticket leases may still be planned and sold in the UK, but the lease agreement is typically written elsewhere for tax reasons.

#Market

Bill of Sale

An historically more commonly used document, which transfers ownership of goods from one person (A) to another in circumstances where A retains possession and use of the goods.

Bills of Sale are also a way in which individuals can treat goods they already own as security for a loan or other obligations, while retaining possession and use of those goods – like taking a mortgage in respect of the goods. They are still quite often utilised when individuals finance boats and other vessels.

The Bill of Sale allows a lender to seize assets without a court order on default. Those for motor vehicles include so-called 'logbook loans'. For some assets, such as high-value cars or works of art, they can be used as alternatives to leases. Operates in a similar way to the corporate financial tool called a Chattel mortgage.

Taking security by way of a Bill of Sale is regarded by some as complex, as they are still governed by statutes dating from 1878 and 1882. In September 2014, the government asked the Law Commission to review the Bills of Sale Acts and make recommendations for its reform. The Commission recommended that the Acts should be repealed and replaced with a new "Goods Mortgages Act" and whilst this recommendation formed part of the Queen's speech in 2017, the government decided in May 2018 that it would not introduce legislation at this point in time, citing a small and reducing market and the wider work on high-cost credit.

Similar attempts at modernising legislation in Scotland resulted in the Moveable Transactions (Scotland) Act 2023 being passed by the Scottish Parliament in May 2023. The act introduced a new form of security that can be granted over Scottish moveable property, the 'Statutory Pledge'. Two registers will be set up by Registers of Scotland, the Register of Assignations, and the Register of Statutory Pledges. The Act is expected to help businesses to raise loans, including asset finance.

#Alternatives

Blind discount

An arrangement whereby a manufacturer or supplier of Assets subsidises the cost of the Assets to be leased, without the customer being made aware of this. The subsidy reduces the price actually paid for the asset by the leasing company. This can enable the lessor to offer a lower or even zero percent (commonly known as an 'Interest Free') deal to the customer. Care is needed for regulated agreements to ensure compliance with APR regulations.

#Market

Blockchain

An electronic register that is shared between at least three users, and often many more. Each copy of the register shows the same information. The register is secure, and transactions cannot be changed once recorded. All parties must agree before a new transaction is added.

Many see potential for use of blockchain in leasing. It might, for example, expedite the preparation of Big-ticket lease agreements that may involve many different parties (e.g. lawyers, accountants, tax specialists and maintenance companies in addition to the lessee and lessor themselves).

#Market

Block discounting

Where a lessor sells the rights to multiple finance agreements (including the right to receive all the customer payments under those finance agreements) that are aggregated in a 'block', to a larger finance company, usually a specialist division of that company.

The portfolio being sold will comprise agreements meeting agreed criteria, such as periods, values, assets, and customer credit risk rating. The purchaser will usually insist that the seller keeps an interest in all agreements, for example selling a maximum percentage from 80% to 95% of the total value of the receivables.

The arrangement is usually undisclosed to the customers as all dealings with the customer - including the work to 'bill and collect' payments' - will continue to be the responsibility of the seller. The technique is used by smaller lessors including brokers wishing to grow their own book. For the originator, the block facility releases invested portfolio capital and enables access to more capital for lending than may otherwise be the case.

#Funding

Book value

The value at which an asset is reported (or 'carried') on a balance sheet. See Capitalised value.

#Accounting

Bond

A debt security that obligates the issuer to pay the security's face value amount on a specified future date in addition to interest payments. Bonds are commonly used by large lessors, mainly in the US and Far East, to raise capital for lending. They are also used by lessors in some European countries, including Germany and Italy.

Access to funding using bonds typically requires a well-established platform, a diversified portfolio and sound credit policies and procedures. Moodys and Standard & Poors have specialist teams that assess investment grades for European lessors. Bonds for asset finance companies are examples of Asset Backed Securities. They are also called debt notes.

#Funding

Borrower

In general terms, anyone who owes money to the finance company, but for asset finance, a more precise term is lessee. The terms is more often used where there is a loan rather than lease.

#Market

Break Option

Where a lease agreement allows the lessee to cancel the agreement on certain dates (the 'break date'), at a pre-defined cost. Few lease agreements include such clauses.

#Contracts

British Bankers' Association (BBA)

Until 2017, the association of banks based in, or with branches in, the UK. The BBA merged with other trade associations to form UK Finance.

#Associations

British Business Bank (BBB)

UK government-owned institution that aims to make finance markets work better for small and medium-sized businesses (SMEs).

It launched in 2014 with an initial £1 billion of government funding. It runs a variety of schemes and programmes, including some previously operated by the Department for Business and Trade and its subsidiary Capital for Enterprise Limited.

The BBB is not an authorised banking institution and hence all its operations work through finance company partners including

a range of lessors. Non-bank lessors may borrow from the BBB through the ENABLE funding mechanism. Lessors may also obtain a government-backed portfolio guarantee in return for a fee through the ENABLE guarantee programme. The Recovery Loan Scheme, formerly the Enterprise Finance Guarantee, provides guarantees for individual loans including asset finance.
www.british-business-bank.co.uk

#Bodies

British Vehicle Rental and Leasing Association (BVRLA)

The trade body for companies engaged in the rental and leasing of cars and commercial vehicles. Established in 1967, it has around 500 member companies offering vehicle rental, contract hire and lease, and fleet management. There are also 330 vehicle leasing brokers. BVRLA members own 2.5 million cars, vans, and trucks. The BVRLA promotes the interests of the sector, has a code of conduct, and operates a conciliation service for its members and their customers to help resolve disputes.
www.bvrla.co.uk

#Associations

Broker

An intermediary who arranges transactions between lessees and lessors. There are at least 500 asset finance broking firms in the UK, including both specialists and general commercial finance brokers who can arrange asset finance alongside other types of finance.

Most finance brokers earn an introductory commission from lessors as opposed to charging the customer a finder's fee.

The majority of asset finance brokers are regulated by the Financial Conduct Authority to permit them to broker regulated agreements, but others deal only with limited companies and do not require authorisation. Some lenders will deal only with FCA-authorised brokers, but others are content to deal with other firms provided they do not introduce regulated customers.

 # Intermediaries

Business Debtline

Run by the charity Money Advice Trust, offering free online debt advice for the self-employed and small businesses. It has a fact sheet on hire purchase and conditional sale and helps businesses to apply for Time orders to reschedule payments or to terminate agreements. Another charity, StepChange, provides similar services to individual consumers. *www.businessdebtline.org*

#Credit

Business risk

The uncertainty faced by a business due to factors specific to its own business, such as changes in the marketplace, reduced sales, or profitability. Part of the overall assessment of the risk of lending.

#Risk

Buy-back

Where a lessor arranges with the supplier to buy back the assets at the end of the lease. Also known as Repuchase agreement. Some captive finance companies have a buy-back arrangement with their parent manufacturers. The technique is also used by vendor finance specialist lessors working with very well-established equipment manufacturers. A risk to the lessor is that the supplier ceases trading during the period of the lease.

Various alternatives can be used instead of the supplier buying back all assets in full. For example, the supplier might guarantee to buy back a certain proportion of assets, possibly those with the highest value (a 'top slice' position). See Call option and Put option.

#Assets

C

Call option

Where a supplier of Assets has the right to buy back the Assets it sold to a lessor for use by a particular lessee at a specified price.

The option would typically be available at the end of the lease agreement or in the event of repossession of the Assets following a default. Not a common arrangement.

#Assets

Capital adequacy

The minimum amount of capital that banks are required to hold in proportion to their risk-adjusted assets.

The rules distinguish between 'tier one' and 'tier two' capital. Tier one is core capital that is relatively transparent and secure, including equity and reserves. Tier two capital is less reliable capital, including categories such as revaluation reserves. Depending on their size, banks have various requirements to hold tier one and total capital equivalent to a percentage of their risk-weighted assets (RWAs).

RWAs reflect the value of assets, the Probability of default (PD), and the expected Loss given default (LGD) for different asset categories. Banks can either adopt 'standardised' risk weightings that are issued by the Prudential Regulation Authority based on the Capital Requirement Directive or may use internal models of risk if approved by the PRA.

Leaseurope research has shown that leasing is much lower risk than other types of lending to businesses. The standardised approach does not distinguish between different types of small business lending, although there is a lower risk weighting for all 'retail' (including small business) exposures.

A lessor able to demonstrate that leasing is very low risk through an approved internal model can benefit from holding less capital than a competitor using the standardised risk weightings, reducing its cost of funding for leasing business. This does require very strong data sets. Few banks do, in practice, distinguish between different leasing and other SME lending products in their capital adequacy models. For this reason, the key effect of the capital adequacy regime tends to be on competition between lessors, rather than competition between leasing and alternative financial products.

#Prudential

Capital allowances

The amount of asset depreciation that can be offset against taxable profits, reducing the amount of tax paid. Accounting depreciation is not allowable as an expense when calculating tax. Instead, firms calculate an alternative value, based on HMRC's capital allowance rules.

Capital allowances are calculated annually as a percentage of the initial cost of the equipment in the first year, or the written-down value at the end of the previous tax year in each subsequent year. There is a balancing allowance or charge when the asset is disposed of. If the actual value at disposal is higher or lower than the amount the tax calculations had estimated, the allowance against tax for that year is adjusted accordingly.

In general, for hire purchase and most finance leases the lessee claims the capital allowances and for most operating leases it is the lessor.

Special (higher) rates apply to some investments including Annual Investment Allowance and Enhanced Capital Allowances.

#Tax

Capital charges

A now defunct public sector accounting term but one that still helps explain attitudes to leasing in the public sector.

Public sector bodies used to use cash accounting techniques and did not maintain balance sheets. This led to concerns that National Health Service hospital trusts and other bodies were not managing their assets efficiently. To address this, the capital charge was introduced in the NHS from 1992 and extended across the public sector from 2000. The charge was a proxy for the cost of capital spent on assets and asset depreciation. It was applied to leased as well as owned assets, arguably overstating the true cost of leasing.

NHS Trusts and other parts of the public sector now use balance sheets and report depreciation rather than the capital charge.

#Public sector

Capital employed

Sum of all money tied up in a business, including fixed assets and working capital. For details of how this is calculated under accounting rules, see Capitalised value. However, regardless of the accounting, a key benefit of leasing is the ability to obtain use of assets without having to find the cash to buy the asset.

#Accounting

Capital expenditure

Investment on fixed assets by a company. A key benefit of leasing is the ability to obtain use of assets without incurring the up-front capital expenditure. Capital-intensive businesses require large investments in capital assets, and therefore high capital expenditure, if leasing is not used.

#Accounting

Capital markets

The markets in which businesses can raise debt and equity finance.

#Funding

Capitalised value

For lease accounting, leases are 'capitalised', or reported as an asset at Book value, by either the lessee or the lessor.

Under traditional lessee accounting rules (IAS 17 and UK Financial Reporting Standards ("FRS") until 2026), at the start of a finance lease the lessee capitalises the present value of the future lease payments but does not capitalise an operating lease asset The lessor capitalises the lease payments due from the lessee for finance leases, and the cost of the assets included in the lease, together with any qualifying expenses, for operating leases.

Under IFRS 16, and UK FRS from 2026, the lessee capitalises the present value of the future lease payments for all leases, at the start of the lease. Lessor accounting is unchanged, i.e. the lessor capitalises the lease payments due from the lessee for finance leases, and the cost of the assets included in the lease, together with any qualifying expenses, for operating leases. As a result, both the lessee and lessor capitalise values associated with former operating leases.

#Accounting

Captive lessor

A lessor whose principal purpose is to provide leasing facilities for the products of the related manufacturer or supplier. May be a subsidiary of the manufacturer or a joint venture with a leasing company or bank. It may lend using its manufacturer parent's own funds or may raise funds in the capital markets.

#Market

Captives forum

Grouping of captive finance companies that seeks to promote the best possible trading conditions for captives across Europe. The Forum is managed by an executive committee of leaders of captives and holds quarterly meetings.
www.captivesforum.org

#Associations

Carry forward

The ability to defer tax allowances, including capital allowances and loss reliefs, from one year to another. This is useful if a company has no, or limited, taxable profits to offset in a particular year. There are restrictions on the proportion of banks' annual taxable profit that can be offset by carried forward losses.

#Tax

Cashflow

The actual cash inflows and outflows of cash faced by a business, which will typically vary from the figures prepared following accounting principles for the firm's profit and loss account.

A key benefit of leasing is in helping businesses to manage their cashflow whilst obtaining the use of assets critical to their success.

Part of lessors' credit analysis process is to establish that a business can afford lease payments, based not only on their accounting profitability but also their ability to find the cash to make the lease payments. A cashflow forecast might be requested from the business for this purpose.

#Credit #Finance

Challenger banks

Relatively newly established and authorised banks, which compete with the long-established large banks. A minority have launched asset finance divisions, typically relying on broker introductions. Recent examples offering asset finance include Allica Bank and Oxbury Bank.

#Market

Chartered Institute of Credit Management (CICM)

The main professional body for the credit community, granted the Royal Charter in 2014. It trains and offers qualifications for professionals working in credit and collections functions mainly in non-financial businesses. Many decision makers or decision influencers in companies using or considering leasing are CICM members. It has published a guide to leasing with the FLA and NACFB, 'Investing in equipment', which explains the benefits as well as some possible risks of leasing.
www.cicm.com

#Bodies

Chattel mortgage

Typically used (for example) with a fixed-term loan for the acquisition of, and secured against, an item of property other than land. The customer owns the asset from the start and pays regular periodic payments for the duration of the agreement.

A Chattel mortgage is a form of security interest, typically a legal mortgage, taken over tangible movable property (known as chattels), to which the party giving the chattel mortgage (the 'mortgagor') has legal title. Such chattels may include plant and machinery, vehicles, and artwork.

Legal title to the chattel (or chattels) is transferred to the mortgagee (typically the lender/funder) on the condition that such title will be transferred back to the mortgagor (who may be the borrower or a third party) upon repayment of the debt.

#Alternatives

CIFAS

The UK's fraud prevention service for the financial services industry. Its mission is to deter, detect and prevent fraud and related financial crime. CIFAS runs a database of confirmed fraud cases. The database helps lessors to identify connections with current customers or new applications. CIFAS members can access the database directly. The credit reference agencies also reflect CIFAS cases in their credit reports. Information on suspected fraud cases in the leasing industry is shared separately, see D&B.
www.cifas.org.uk

#Risk

Circular economy

The antidote to modern society's 'take, make and dispose' economic model. It is an economy in which assets are designed to be repaired, reused, or recycled, not disposed of.

Leasing can be an enabler of the circular economy. Lessors can promote leasing of equipment that is likely to retain its value, find new customers for refurbished off-lease equipment, and may work with manufacturers to facilitate the remanufacture, or recycling of obsolete equipment. See 'Leasing-as-a-service'.

#Market #ESG

Claims Management Company (CMC)

A company that offers a service for people or firms seeking to claim compensation, including for mis-sold financial products and services.

CMCs have been particularly prominent in relation to PPI mis-selling and, more recently, in relation to motor finance discretionary commission arrangements. A few CMCs have also tried to sell their services to lessees, including schools that might have Ultra vires leases (i.e. leases entered into without requisite authority). In general, they have limited success, but they can still lead to considerable cost and disruption for lessors.

CMCs are regulated by the FCA, and if they handle consumer litigation claims, they also need to be approved by the Solicitors Regulation Authority.

#Risk

Clawbacks

Where a leasing broker is obliged to repay some or all its commission to the lessor in certain circumstances, for example, if the lease agreement goes into default within the first year.

#Intermediaries

Club loan

A loan from a small syndicate of banks. Non-bank lessors might raise finance using a club loan facility although it is unusual. A challenge with such an arrangement is obtaining a consistent approach to the facility from the participating banks. From a credit lending and deal structuring perspective the facility risk rests with the originating lessor. The banking syndicate may take security over the company's portfolio.

#Funding

Collateral risk

For lessors, the risk that where additional collateral is taken, for example directors' guarantees or Liens against personal or business assets, it will prove to be less valuable than expected if it has to be called upon.

For funding, where a lessor issues Asset-backed securities, the risk to investors that the cashflows from the underlying portfolio of leases will not materialise or will fall short of the amounts required.

#Funding #Risk

Collaterised lease equipment obligations

An American term for Asset-backed securities where receivables from portfolios of equipment assets provide the security.

#Funding

Collections

Usually refers to the activities of a specialist team in handling lease agreements in arrears, either internal to the lessor or to an external debt collection agency. The referral of lease contracts to a collections team should achieve the joint objectives of helping to recover the debt and ensuring compliance with industry best practices and regulations, including (as relevant) the detailed FCA rules affecting regulated agreements.

#Credit

Comfort letters

Typically, a written assurance provided by a parent company in respect of a subsidiary's financial obligations to a lender or lessor. Comfort letters are not usually intended to be legally binding but may give rise to a legal obligation depending on the drafting.

See also Side-letter.

#Contracts #Risk

Commercial CAIS

A database run by Experian that shows smaller businesses' track record in paying for their credit agreements. Finance companies, including many lessors, supply information on their customers and may access the information provided by other members. Information shared includes the start date and length of the agreement, credit outstanding and whether payments have been made on time.

The data is shared with other credit reference agencies under arrangements overseen by a cross industry group, the Steering Committee on Reciprocity (SCOR). The lessee's agreement is required before their records can be shared. The parallel CAIS system holds information on individuals' credit agreements.

#Credit

Commissions

Cash payments or other rewards paid by lessors to brokers, suppliers, or any other intermediaries.

Commissions are typically set at either a rate fixed by the lender, or using a a 'Difference in Charges' model, where the lessor quotes the interest rate it is willing to offer finance at, and the broker adds a commission margin to this. Both options have advantages and disadvantages.

A fixed rate can cause brokers to lose business prospects, when they would be happy to accept a lower commission to win the business, although this can be managed by allowing brokers to reduce their commission from the standard amount. A fixed rate can also make it difficult or uneconomic for a broker to handle more complicated customer requirements.

A Difference in Charges approach provides the broker with more flexibility to match the commission to the work involved. Lenders typically set a maximum rate, but in a competitive market brokers will typically set prices much lower than this.

For regulated motor finance lending, the FCA banned Difference in Charges commissions models in 2021 (see Difference in Charges commissions). Although the ban did not extend to other types of assets, the FCA noted that its rules require lenders to ensure that where brokers can earn different commissions, the differences are justified by level of work required.

Many lessors now set fixed rates for all business or fixed rates with an option to charge less and take a lower commission.

#Intermediaries

Commitment letter

Document which confirms a lessor's intention to enter into a lease agreement (for example) with a lessee. It is drawn up before the lease agreement is signed and sets out the headline terms of the proposed lease agreement.

It is typically used for large transactions, such as aircraft leases, where the lessor might be required to incur expenses before the full details of the lease are ready to agree. It can be stated that it is not legally binding, but in general the lessee could be liable to pay damages if they were to walk away, i.e. not agree or sign the proposed lease agreement but that would depend on the specific terms of the Commitment letter.

A commitment fee may be payable by the lessee to the lessor at the time the lessee signs the letter. This is akin to a deposit.

#Contracts

Common law

The legal system governing England and Wales, a system characterised by judicial precedents of cases brought before the courts whose judges interpret legislation (e.g. acts of Parliament, or international laws). Common law establishes, for example, that a lease with no transfer of ownership of the Assets is a contract of bailment, and a lease agreement may be illegal if the Assets are to be used for illegal purposes.

#Legal

Conditional sale

A lease that is a credit agreement in legal terms (not hire) as ownership of the asset transfers automatically to the lessee at the end of the term, if the lessee has met all the conditions. Unlike hire purchase, transfer of ownership is not reliant on an option to purchase being exercised by the hirer.

#Products

Conduct of business

For consumer credit regulated business, the Consumer Credit Sourcebook (CONC) section of the FCA Handbook. There are rules covering financial promotions, pre-contractual requirements, responsible lending, arrears, defaults, and recovery. Some rules apply only to credit, others to hire and credit. Some apply to all regulated firms, others to either brokers, hirers, or lenders.

#Conduct

Construction & Agricultural Equipment Security and Registration Scheme (CESAR)

A secure labelling system for plant and machinery, backed by the Construction Equipment Association and the Agricultural Engineers Association and operated by Datatag.

Many farm and construction equipment manufacturers fit CESAR identification during the production process. In addition to visible tamper-proof identification plates the system encompasses hidden transponders and DNA labelling.

The scheme aims to cut theft of construction plant and agricultural machinery by reducing reliance on traditional registration or serial number plates which are relatively easy to alter. Lessors can register their ownership of equipment fitted with CESAR plates on HPI allowing their interest to be seen in provenance checks by other finance companies and the police.
www.cesarscheme.org

#Risk

Consumables

The often mundane items that are needed when using leased assets, such as toner for printers and food and drinks in Vending machines. For convenience, some leases may come bundled with a supply of consumables. The lessee needs to be confident that the quantities being supplied are suitable, the arrangement will represent good value for its duration, and the period of the supply of consumables is no longer than the term of the lease.

There have been incidents where consumables have been offered to a customer free of charge by a supplier, either on an undocumented basis or through a side-letter. This can be risky for both lessee and lessor as the supplier may not provide the consumables.

#Contracts #Risk

Consumer credit

lease agreements regulated under the UK's Consumer Credit Act and the Financial Services and Markets Act. The regulator for consumer credit is the Financial Conduct Authority (FCA). Most credit or hire products, including all leasing, are regulated when provided to individuals, unincorporated businesses, or unincorporated partnerships of 2 or 3 partners. A wide range of activities involved in consumer credit are regulated, including broking and dealing with the debts of regulated customers.

Most of the asset finance market is not regulated for consumer credit purposes. Around 70% of small businesses are companies and are not regulated and that proportion has been growing in recent years. Only 5% of asset finance business users are likely to be FCA-regulated and around 2% of the market by value. The regulation is, however, particularly important in agricultural equipment leasing and in professions such as design and architecture, where many firms are unincorporated.

Although only a small part of the market, any lessors or intermediaries wishing to serve regulated customers must register with the FCA and comply with its Rulebook. Some of the FCA's rules apply across the business, not only when dealing with regulated customers.

#Conduct #Legal

Consumer Credit Act 1974 (CCA)

Legislation that governs agreements with unincorporated bodies where the transaction is non-exempt. Exemptions may apply to agreements over £25,000 for business use and to high net worth individuals. Some parts of the Act have been incorporated into the FCA's Handbook and have been repealed but other parts (the 'retained provisions') remain in place.

In 2022, the government announced its intention to reform the CCA to ensure it is fit for purpose and keeps pace with technological advancements and changing consumer needs. Following an initial consultation in 2022, the Government had planned to issue a second-stage consultation in 2024 but this did not happen before the General Election, which took place in July 2024.

Some have argued that the opportunity should be taken to remove business transactions from this legislation that is designed to protect consumers, which would be a major shift in policy.

#Conduct #Legal

Consumer Credit Sourcebook (CONC)

See Conduct of Business.

#Conduct

Consumer Duty

In 2023, the FCA introduced new rules and an additional principle, setting out higher and clearer standards of consumer protection across financial services, and requiring regulated firms to put their customers' needs first, to ensure good customer outcomes.

For asset finance, which is typically a straightforward financial solution provided to business users who are likely to already be familiar with the arrangements, the new rules typically involved refining existing policies and procedures, rather than any fundamental changes. Some changes were often needed, however, including:

- Lessors providing intermediaries with information about their products, including the target market and the lessor's assessment of how the product offers 'fair value' to customers in the target market.
- Reviewing website and other content to ensure it is as clear as possible to customers in the relevant target markets.
- Introduction or expansion of customer surveys, to confirm regulated lessees understand the information that has been

provided to them, are able to make good decisions, and are happy with the services provided to them.
- For intermediaries, maintaining records to justify the selection of a particular lessor (or group of lessors with similar rates, sometimes called 'Tiers').

Regulated firms are required to review their compliance with Consumer Duty rules annually.

#Conduct

Consumer Credit Trade Association (CCTA)

Founded in 1891, the CCTA is the trade organisation for firms specialising in consumer lending. It started life as the Hire Traders Protection Association, became the Hire Purchase Trade Association in 1949, and then the CCTA in 1978. Some smaller lessors including brokers with own books join the CCTA to obtain practical support with their consumer credit activities including access to model credit agreements that are compliant with the relevant legislation. *www.ccta.co.uk*

#Associations

Consumer Rights Act 2015 (the 'CRA')

The Consumer Rights Act 2015 applies to consumers entering into lease/hire, lease/hire purchase and conditional sale agreements. The CRA provides that all Assets under such agreements must be of satisfactory quality, fit for purpose and as described, and provides consumers with rights and remedies if the Assets do not meet those standards.

#Legal

Container leasing

Since the first use of containers for moving cargo in the 1950s, the container industry has grown to over 37 million TEUs today. A TEU is a twenty-foot equivalent unit, so a smaller container of 20 foot is one TEU, a large container of 40 foot is two TEUs. 20 million TEUs are leased together with 550,000 of the chassis units that hold them. The replacement value of the leased fleet is estimated at US$53billion. A host of domestic and international laws, regulations, conventions and standards apply to this most international of industries.

The International Institute of Container Lessors is based in Washington DC and represents a dozen of the largest global lessors. *www.iicl.org*

#Market

Contingent rentals

Lease payments that vary depending on factors defined in the lease agreement, such as the level of use of the asset.

#Accounting #Contract

Continuation

For lease accounting, a lease is assumed to be non-cancellable if the cost to the lessee to cancel is such that continuation of the lease is reasonably certain. More generally, the term can also refer to a lease entering a secondary period.

#Accounting #Contract

Contract hire

A lease agreement, typically for cars, which is bundled with services. For company car fleets the services might include maintenance, insurance, replacement vehicles and fleet administration. As it is a hire agreement, the assets are returned to the lessor at the end of the agreed period. For car fleets there will typically still be a substantial residual value, making the accuracy of forecasting used car prices critical to contract hire pricing and profitability.

#Products

Conversion rate

Proportion of quotations that are accepted and result in a lease contract being made.

#Operations

Corporate guarantee

Where another company, often the parent company of the lessee, guarantees to pay amounts that become due under a lease if the lessee fails to do so. Like a Personal guarantee, it can sometimes enable lessors to fund equipment that would otherwise be declined.

#Credit

Corporate interest restriction rules

Tax rules, introduced in 2017 in the UK and across Europe, which restrict the interest cost that multinational companies may deduct from taxable profits. The rules are complex, but broadly limit interest expense to 30% of earnings before tax. This could affect the tax deductibility of interest on finance leases, but the threshold is so high that UK lessees are unlikely to be affected.

#Tax

Corporation tax

Taxes paid by companies on their taxable profits. Taxable profits are based on accounting profit with various adjustments. Accounting depreciation is not allowable as an expense for tax purposes but instead tax capital allowances may be claimed.

#Tax

Cost / income

Operating expenses as a percentage of operating income. In the Leaseurope Index, the weighted average of all participating companies' cost/income ratios in 2023 was 46%. For the Leaseurope Index operating expenses excludes interest, and operating income includes net interest.

#Operations

Cost of capital

The cost of a firm's finance, calculated as a weighted average of debt and equity (also known as Weighted Average Cost of Capital). The higher a firm's cost of capital, the more likely it is that leasing assets will be an attractive option. This is one reason lease penetration rates for large listed companies are low on average but also vary considerably between firms.

#Finance

Cost of risk

Loan loss provisions as a percentage of average portfolio. In the Leaseurope Index, the average cost of risk for participating companies in 2023 was 0.2%, while Asset Finance Policy analysis showed a median cost of risk for UK lessors of 1.1%.

The balance of provisions is different from the annual cost charged to the profit and loss (income) statement, which reflects only the net movement in the balance after write-offs, new provisions and any other adjustments.

The difference between the Leaseurope and UK numbers may in part reflect the inclusion of mainly large banks in the European numbers with low-risk portfolios, compared to a wider range of lessors in the UK with a wider range of risk appetites.

#Risk

Co-terminous agreement

Where two or more leases start on different dates but finish on the same date. This may happen if, for example, a lessee wishes to add some extra cars to its fleet. It is more commonly found in the property rather than equipment leasing market.

#Contracts

County Court Judgement (CCJ)

A court ruling from the County Court (England & Wales and Northern Ireland) in favour of a creditor claiming that monies owed have not been paid. It applies to both individuals and companies. Once the court order has been registered and is in the public domain, credit reference agencies will use this information to reassess creditworthiness. CCJs may therefore have a negative impact on the credit rating of an individual or company with a CCJ against them.

#Risk

Covenants

A clause in a contract that contains a restriction or a requirement or a commitment that certain acts will be performed. Bank loans may include financial covenants requiring borrowers to maintain minimum ratios of assets to liabilities or that restrict the firm's absolute level of liabilities.

In a lease agreement, the term can also refer more generally to the lessee's obligations e.g. to make rental payments and to maintain the assets.

#Contracts

Credit

Any kind of loan or other 'financial accommodation' that provides a right to defer repayment for goods or services or for lending of money. This includes any leasing agreement where the lessee has an option to buy the asset from the lessor. The purchase option can be set out in the lease agreement or separately. If there is no such option in a lease, the agreement will generally be one of hire and not credit.

#Conduct #Legal

Credit institution

Under European law, an authorised financial institution. A Capital Requirements Directive (CRD) credit institution is one that accepts deposits or other funds from the public and grants credits and is subject to prudential regulation. Details vary by country, but in general a non-CRD credit institution is one that does not take deposits but is still subject to prudential regulation.

In the UK, non-bank lessors are not required to be authorised for prudential purposes, other than a notional prudential requirement for firms that are authorised by the FCA to carry out regulated consumer credit activities.

#Prudential

Credit line

A commitment in principle by a lessor to allow a customer to take out multiple lease agreements up to a defined limit. The credit limit can be a one-off facility with a fixed maximum, or a more flexible 'revolving' arrangement allowing the customer to reduce their borrowings and then increase them again. Unless the customer's circumstances have changed, or there are any particularly unusual characteristics of the asset or supplier, the customer can expect each application to be accepted.

#Credit

Credit loss

For accounting, the difference between the contracted and expected cashflows, including the lease rentals and any other income that is part of the credit provided. For IFRS 9, a loss allowance is made for this amount in the accounts. 12-month Expected Credit Losses ("12m ECL") is the proportion of lifetime expected credit losses that will probably be realised within the next 12 months.

#Accounting

Credit rating

An independent assessment of a company's creditworthiness. For the largest companies it is based on an expert assessment. For smaller companies it is typically an automated assessment based on available electronic data. It may be referred to as a 'credit score' or 'credit report' rather than credit rating. As most small companies now file only abbreviated accounts at Companies House the credit reference agencies tend to rely on non-accounting data when preparing credit reports.

#Credit

Credit risk

The possibility that a lessee could default on lease rental payments, leaving the lessor having to consider recovering and selling the asset or taking legal action to recover the amount owed.

#Credit #Risk

Credit sale

The sale of an asset with extended credit provided by the supplier. An alternative to leasing but found mainly in the consumer goods markets.

#Alternatives

Cross-border leasing

Contract where the lessee and lessor are in different countries, includes export leasing. Often, but not necessarily, the leased assets will be located in the lessee's home country.

#Market

Crowdfunding

A form of Alternative finance, where a project is financed through small investments from many people, typically arranged using an online portal.

It has been suggested that crowdfunding could disrupt the leasing market, reducing the importance of banks and even making it possible to offer leasing arrangements that might be considered too risky today, but there have been no signs of this happening.

#Alternatives

Crown Commercial Service (CCS)

An executive agency of the Government, sponsored by the Cabinet Office, which advises the public sector on procurement and carries out central purchasing on behalf of multiple departments.

It is the latest in a line of efforts to improve the efficiency of public procurement, following the Government Procurement Service (GPS) and Buying Solutions.

The CCS's framework RM3781 provides customers across the whole of the public sector with access to multifunctional devices (MFDs) such as printers and photocopiers, managed print and records information management services, including related finance options. Contract RM3710 covers vehicle leasing and associated services including fleet management. Contact RM6146 covers leasing advisory services. Central Government departments are under increasing pressure to use the CCS-negotiated contracts to exploit the full potential buying power of the public sector.

#Public sector

D

Data protection

The regulations over how firms protect the privacy of individuals set out in the Data Protection Act 2018, which incorporate the requirements of the European Union's General Data Protection Regulations. Lessors need to register annually as data controllers with the Information Commissioner's Office if they are obtaining, recording, storing, updating and sharing personal information on individuals from lessees' businesses. See General Data Protection Regulation.

#Regulation

Dealer

Firms, other than manufacturers, which sell vehicles or equipment to businesses or individuals. They may offer finance options to their customers, either by introducing them to a finance company or through a broker. The term is typically used in the office equipment sector. See also Resellers.

#Intermediaries

Debenture

A type of loan agreement to a company that is registered at Companies House and gives the lender security over the borrower's assets. The debenture can include either a floating charge over a range of assets, or a fixed charge over a particular asset (typically property, or plant and machinery fixed to the floor). It is not usually relevant where the ownership of the asset will remain with the lessor but may be used when providing asset based finance.

#Risk

Debt adjusting

For consumer credit regulation, the regulated activity of negotiating with a lender or owner, on behalf of a borrower or hirer, the settlement of a regulated credit or hire agreement. Firms carrying out debt adjusting in the consumer credit market require specific FCA permission. Obtaining a settlement figure for an existing asset finance agreement on behalf of a regulated customer is generally considered to be debt adjusting, but not advising customers on how to obtain a settlement figure themselves.

#Conduct

Debt counselling

For consumer credit regulation, the regulated activity of giving advice to a borrower about the settlement of a debt due under a credit agreement or giving advice to a hirer about the settlement of a debt due under a consumer hire agreement. Firms carrying out debt counselling in the consumer credit market require specific FCA permission. Setting out options available to the customer in a neutral way such that no advice or opinion is provided is not debt counselling.

#Conduct

Debtor

Any person that owes money, including a lessee's committed lease payments to a lessor, and a borrower's committed loan payments to a lender.

#Market

Default

Failure to meet the terms of an agreement, for example not making lease payments. Under prudential accounting rules, the classification of agreements as being in default needs to consider the number of days past due (as a starting point, 90 days is often used) as well as the likeliness of the customer to pay.

#Credit

Default interest

Where a higher rate of interest is charged to a borrower who is in arrears. This is not common practice in leasing although a late payment fee may be charged by some lessors.

#Credit #Contracts

Deferred taxation

A deferred tax liability is an accounting provision for tax that is not due to be paid within the current year but may have to be paid at some future time. A deferred tax asset is a possible right to pay less tax in the future. For some lessors, including those with long-life assets such as railway rolling stock, significant deferred tax assets have arisen in the past through capital allowances carried forward from the year in which leased equipment was acquired.

#Accounting #Tax

Delinquent receivable

Payments that are overdue but not yet classed as defaulted. More commonly referred to as arrears. The expectation may still be that the amounts due will eventually be paid off.

#Credit

Department for Business and Trade (DBT)

The government department for economic growth. It aims to support businesses to invest, grow and export, creating jobs and opportunities across the UK. It owns the British Business Bank, although the BBB has operational independence.

It has been through various reorganisations and names including the Department for Business, Innovation and Skills before 2016, then the Department for Business, Energy and Industrial Strategy from 2016 to 2023.

#Bodies

Deposit

A payment made at the outset of a lease agreement which reduces the amount funded. The ongoing lease payments should be lower than if there was no deposit. Sometimes called an 'initial payment'. It serves to mitigate the lessor's risk caused by many assets being worth substantially less as soon as they are no longer new. See also Security deposit.

#Contracts

Depreciation

The reduction in an asset's value over time. Depreciation is charged as an operating expense in the lessee's income statement for assets under a finance lease, or the lessor's income statement for an operating lease. The two main methods of calculating depreciation are straight-line and reducing balance. The aim of either method is to realistically reflect the asset's current value to the business.

#Accounting

Difference in Charges commission

A method for calculating the commission paid to a broker by a lender (see Commissions). There are two variants.

Under an 'increasing Difference in Charges' model the lender sets a minimum charge rate for the proposed lease. The broker adds a margin to this to reach the charge rate to be quoted to the customer. In general, the difference between the two charge rates is the broker's commission.

A 'reducing Difference in Charges' commission is where the lender sets a maximum interest rate, and the broker can choose whether to quote that to the customer or to reduce the rate (and earn less commission) to be more competitive.

The 'increasing' approach can be seen as controversial and has attracted some attention from the FCA for regulated consumer car finance agreements, as it creates a theoretical incentive for the broker to mislead a customer about the rates available in the market.

This potential conflict has largely been addressed by lenders either shifting to the 'reducing' model or imposing caps on the 'increasing' charge rate to customers. The competitive market also imposes a natural limit on rates that can be charged to lessees.

The Financial Conduct Authority banned the use of Difference in Charges commissions for motor finance in 2021.

#Conduct #Intermediaries

DIMS

Durable, Identifiable, Moveable and Saleable: The four traditional tests for whether an asset is suitable for leasing. It might be most accurate to identify them now as the tests of whether there is a Hard asset, noting that non-DIMS assets may also be leasable

#Assets

Diploma in Asset Finance

Online course and qualification in asset finance, run by the London Institute of Banking and Finance, and created in conjunction with the Finance and Leasing Association. The qualification is offered as a set of online materials, with three modules expected to take

15 months to study. See Finance Houses Diploma.
www.libf.ac.uk

#Operations

Direct debit

Using a mandate provided by the lessee, the arrangement by which lessors will usually collect lease payments from the lessee's bank account.

#Credit

Direct tax

Another name for corporation tax.

#Tax

Disadvantages of Leasing

As shown under the Advantages of leasing, the benefits of leasing vary between types of leases and the lessee's circumstances. The possible disadvantages to a potential lessee – which are often avoidable by selecting the most appropriate lessor and type of lease – might include:

Higher cost than using retained earnings or bank loans to pay for assets due to any of the following:

- The firm having access to lower cost capital or loans than the interest rate inherent in the lease
- Additional fees and other charges for the lease e.g. administration, documentation, purchase option, renewal and insurance
- The firm having tax capacity, particularly for Annual Investment Allowances, but wishing to use a lease where capital allowances are not available to the lessee
- Having access to similar equipment at lower cost from other suppliers not offering leasing options.

Non-pricing lease terms that might not suit the potential lessee's needs if not carefully selected:

- The risk that the firm will have to return equipment it still needs at the end of the lease if there is no purchase option, or if the terms of the option are unattractive, or if the contract is not fully understood
- An end-date of the lease, or absence of a specific end-date, which could lead to a firm having to pay for equipment it might no longer need
- Conditions for returning equipment at end of lease that might be difficult to meet.

Risks arising from associated parties:

- Accepting offers (in Comfort or Side-letters) of additional benefits from intermediaries that might not actually be delivered, possibly leading to conflict between the contracting parties.
- Paying in advance for services or maintenance by third parties that might not ultimately be delivered

#Alternatives

Disclosed agency

See Agency agreement.

#Legal

Discount rate

The interest rate used to calculate a discounted cash flow. The rate is applied to future cash flows to state them in current prices. The discount rate seeks to remove the time value of money from future cash flows.

#Finance

Discounted cash flow

The present value of a series of future cash flow e.g. lease payments, calculated by applying a discount rate to the payments. It can be used in a lease vs. buy analysis for example. If a firm has surplus cash, a relevant rate might reflect the alternative ways in which that money could be used. Otherwise the relevant rate could be the cost of borrowing funds to buy, rather than lease, the asset.

#Finance

Distributor

Firm that distributes a manufacturer's goods to suppliers for onward sale to businesses or individuals. The distributor may work with a lessor to establish a vendor finance programme for use by dealers.

#Intermediaries

Double-dip lease

An international lease where, due to different tax rules in different countries, both the lessee and the lessor can claim capital allowances (or equivalent tax benefits) on the same equipment. Many tax authorities have taken steps to stop this happening.

#Tax

Drawdown

Taking just some of the funds from a credit line, block discounting facility or other available facility.

#Contracts

Dual financing

See Multi-financing

#Risk

Due Diligence

Steps taken by lessors to ensure that the information they have been given about any proposed transaction is accurate.

#Risk

Dun & Bradstreet (D&B) Critical Intelligence System

Credit reference agency D&B runs a system allowing lessors to share suspicions on suspicious businesses in a secure and safe environment. Established with support from the FLA and following review of relevant legal aspects, the system is intended to allow the industry to share suspicions on suspected fraudsters and stops them from approaching different lessors until one offers finance. Information filed by participating lessors is also investigated by D&B specialists. The system helps lessors identify when to carry out additional anti-fraud checks. It can also help them to confirm that a business which might initially appear suspicious is genuine.

#Risk

E

e-signatures

A digital equivalent to a 'wet ink' signature on a contract. These are now becoming more commonly used in leasing, especially in the smaller ticket space. Whilst there has been some debate whether e-signatures are capable of meeting the statutory requirements, this is generally accepted by most funders for execution of simple contracts. However, some question marks remain with regards to documents which are executed as deeds e.g. personal guarantees and there are specific legal requirements to consider if signing Scots-law governed or Northern Irish-law governed agreements electronically.

If a contract involves a party outside the UK, it is important to understand whether electronic execution is permissible in that relevant jurisdiction.

#Contracts

Early settlement

Where a lease agreement is cancelled by the lessee before the end of the contracted primary or minimum period.

For a non-regulated credit agreement, the lessor is under no obligation to forego any of the lease payments due. In some circumstances lessors may voluntarily discount the total amount payable to exclude interest charges due for the remaining period of the lease.

For a regulated credit agreement (as defined by the Consumer Credit Act 1974) the lessee may terminate at any time (an 'Early termination'). If the payments made exceed half of the total amount payable, and the asset is in good condition, no further amounts are due. Otherwise the lessee will need to pay the sum needed to bring the total payments to that level.

#Contracts

Earnings before Interest and Tax (EBIT)

One way of measuring and reporting profit. It is often seen as the most useful measure of the underlying performance of a company, as it is not dependent upon changes in interest or tax rates that are outside of the company's control.

A curious effect of new lease accounting rules (IFRS 16 and UK FRS from 2026) is that EBIT increases for lessees, as compared to historical lease accounting rules. This is because in the past, EBIT was calculated after deducting the total expense of operating leases. Under the new rules, the lease cost is split between depreciation and interest, and only the depreciation is deducted when calculating EBIT. In 'real money' (cash) terms, however, nothing has changed.

#Accounting

Economic life

See Useful life.

#Assets

Economic Crime Levy

From 2024, lessors whose UK revenue exceeds £10.2 million per year are required to pay the Economic Crime Levy, which is intended to increase funding for developing the UK's long-term sustainable solution to tackle economic crime.

The levy ranges from £10,000 for medium-sized businesses to £250,000 for very large corporations and is based on total business income. As a result, this can represent a significant extra overhead for some large dealers of assets with relatively small own book leasing operations.

#Regulation

Economic owner

The party that enjoys the benefits of using an asset in its business and accepts the associated risks. Lease accounting and taxation rules have traditionally been based on this concept as opposed to legal ownership.

Although the lessor is the legal owner of leased assets, for finance leases the economic owner is generally considered to be the lessee. As a result, under lessor accounting rules, the lessor does not report the asset on its balance sheet. For tax purposes it is generally the lessee who is eligible to claim capital allowances.

#Accounting #Tax

Educational and Skills Funding Agency (ESFA)

The executive agency of the Department for Education that manages finance for all state schools in England, allocating finance through local authorities as well as direct to academy schools.

The ESFA is particularly relevant for leasing by academy schools, which include around 80% of secondary schools and 45% of primary schools.

The ESFA issues an Academies Financial Handbook which states that academies may use operating leases but must seek ESFA approval before using finance leases. The ESFA has said that it will approve use of finance leases if they represent good value, but in practice few academies appear to have obtained such approval. In effect, therefore, academy schools were restricted to using operating leases, in line with local authority-funded schools.

With the implementation of IFRS 16 in the public sector, ending the distinction between operating and finance leases for accounting purposes, the Government stated in 2024 that under the Education Act 2002, all leases will be classed as borrowing and will require the Secretary of State for Education's consent. However, under new guidance to schools, there is no longer a need for schools to make specific requests for consent where a lease falls The first version of the general consent document in 2024 included a wide range of types of equipment, together with minibuses.

#Bodies #Public sector

Embedded finance

Where finance offers and solutions are integrated into non-financial processes. For asset finance, it is likely to mean that leasing options are offered during the process of ordering assets from suppliers, rather than as a separate process. See Fintech.

#Business

Embezzlement

The theft by the lessee or connected party of a leased asset in situations where the contract may have been entered into lawfully, but a fraud occurs during the life of the contract. This can often happen following a deterioration in the performance of the lessee's business. Embezzlement is a criminal offence.

#Risk

End-of-life functions

Activities to deal with the termination of lease contracts, including settlements or asset disposal.

#Operations

Endorsement

A variation or amendment to a lessor's standard lease agreement terms and conditions. The changes may be specified on a separate sheet or schedule, cross-referenced to the standard agreement and signed and dated by both parties at the same time as the main agreement. Simpler variations may be handled by deletions or amendments initialled by both parties.

#Contracts

Enhanced capital allowances (ECAs)

Where the Government allows businesses to claim Capital allowances more quickly than norma for particular asset types.

ECAs for eligible energy saving and water efficient technologies allow 100% capital allowances in the year of purchase. In 2024, ECAs were available for electric and zero-emissions cars and goods vehicles, plant and machinery for gas refuelling stations, gas, biogas and hydrogen refuelling equipment, equipment for electric vehicle charging points, and plant and machinery for use in a special tax site in UK Freeports or Investment Zones.

The Annual Investment Allowance has the same effect. ECAs are useful for businesses with tax capacity using finance leases and hire purchase. They cannot be claimed by lessors other than for equipment they are using themselves.

#Tax

Equipment Leasing and Finance Association (ELFA)

The Washington DC-based trade association for the $1 trillion US equipment finance sector, including providers of leasing but also loans for buying assets and lines of credit used for equipment purchases. ELFA represents around 575 member companies including national, regional and community banks, other financial services companies and manufacturers providing finance for equipment. In addition to its lobbying work it acts as the central resource for industry information, promotes the industry and is the forum for industry development including through its annual convention.

www.elfaonline.org

#Associations

Equipment Leasing and Finance Foundation

The US-based body that amongst other activities develops and publishes research relevant to the equipment finance industry. Established in 1989 by the Equipment Leasing and Finance Association, its trustees are appointed by the Association. It publishes the Journal of Equipment Lease Financing, State of the Industry reports, a monthly confidence index survey. Its Industry Future Council, comprising a cross-section of selected industry executives, explores current issues, trends, and the outlook for the future of the equipment finance industry.
www.leasefoundation.org

#Associations

Equipment Leasing Association

Set up in 1971 to represent the leasing industry by members of the Finance Houses Association, with which it shared premises and staff. From a base of 13 founder companies it grew to a membership of more than 70 lessors. It merged with the Finance Houses Association in 1992 to form the Finance and Leasing Association ("FLA"). The merger reflected the fact that both the FHA and the ELA were representing the business leasing market, although it left the UK without a dedicated leasing association.

#Associations

Equipment schedule

A document that may supplement a lease agreement especially where multiple items of equipment are involved. It contains details of the specific assets that will be leased, including for example the type of equipment, serial numbers, location and purchase price.

Holding this information on a separate document is done for convenience, allowing the key terms and conditions of the lease to be agreed before the full details of the assets are known.

#Contract

Equity in a lease

The difference between the accounting value of the leased assets and the minimum lease payments owed by the lessee. The equity in a lease should be broadly equivalent to the assets' residual value.

#Accounting

Ethical conduct

General principles that govern standards of behaviour, for example in this context, honesty, trustworthiness, fairness, transparency in responsible lending i.e. looking after the borrower's needs.

Although not labelled as such, the principles making up the FLA Business Finance Code can be seen as defining ethical behaviour in the leasing industry. They include

- Treating customers fairly and follow all relevant laws and regulations.
- Taking reasonable steps to encourage responsible trading between intermediaries and customers.
- Providing customers with appropriate and timely information about the business finance agreement, including the options available at expiry or termination, in a manner which is clear, understandable, and not misleading.
- Providing effective customer service throughout the period of the finance agreement.
- Operating an effective complaints procedure and ensure this is transparent and easily accessible for customers

The FCA handbook, including the Consumer Duty rules, provide further useful guidance on what constitutes ethical behaviour.

Although the principles of ethical behaviour may be clear, making ethical decisions on a day-to-day basis is more complicated. For example, it is right to refer a customer to negative publicity about a competitor? Or is it right to accept introductions from a vendor which has been having quality of service issues?

The starting point in ethical conduct is to recognise the possible issue and consider all arguments.

#Market #Conduct

European Central Bank (ECB)

The central bank of the 19 European Union countries in the Eurozone. Its main task is to maintain price stability and so preserve the purchasing power of the single currency. Under the Single Supervisory Mechanism, from 2014 the ECB has directly supervised the most significant banks in the Eurozone and it oversees the supervision by national regulators of other banks. It is, therefore, the key prudential supervisor for many European bank lessors. The Bank of England and the ECB cooperate to help ensure a consistent approach to bank supervision.
www.ecb.europa.eu

#Bodies #Prudential

European Data Warehouse (EDW)

The European repository for loan-level data for Asset-Backed Securities (ABS) transactions.

For each ABS, it holds information on type of underlying loans, loan size and balance, length of loan and maturity date, interest rate and arrears or losses. The identity of the borrower is not included. The EDW is run by the market and endorsed by the Eurosystem, the collective of the European Central Bank (ECB) and the national central banks (NCBs) of the EU member states that have adopted the euro. For issuers who file information with the EDW their ABS should be eligible as collateral eligible European Central Bank schemes.

Outside of Italy, the EDW is the only repository of shared lease performance information in the EU.

Following Brexit, it is also registered as a UK Securitisation Repository (SR). Public securitisations within the scope of the UK Securitisation Regulation have to upload information to a registered SR.
www.eurodw.eu

#Bodies #Funding

European Financial Reporting Advisory Group (EFRAG)

Association representing a range of European bodies that aims to represent the European public interest during the International Accounting Standards Board's development of changes to international accounting standards. Having earlier been critical of many aspects of the IASB's proposals for a new lease accounting standard, EFRAG eventually advised the European Commission that IFRS 16 was in the European public good, leading to it being approved for use in Europe (including, at the time, the UK).

EFRAG is responsible for the development of European sustainability reporting standards, including banking-specific rules that are due to take effect from 2026 in Europe.
www.efrag.org

#Accounting

European Investment Bank (EIB)

The European Union's Bank. The EIB is owned by the EU member states and provides finance for projects that support EU policy objectives. It borrows on the international capital markets at low rates because of the support provided by the EU national governments.

The EIB supports projects that make a significant contribution to growth and employment in Europe. Its intermediated loans and guarantee schemes are used by many leasing companies in Europe.

The EIB Loans for SMEs programme provides low cost funds to intermediary financial institutions for lending to small and medium-sized businesses. Participating lessors match the funds provided by the EIB, but not necessarily at the same rate. The benefit of the EIB's low cost finance is passed on to the lessee through a lower overall rate for the lease. The rate varies from case to case depending on the credit profile of the lessee or any other party that guarantees the loan, such as a parent bank.

The EIB also provides intermediated loans for other goals including promoting employment amongst mid-cap companies and promoting environmental sustainability.

The EIB credit intermediation programmes had relatively little use in the UK prior to Brexit, and although in theory the EIB could still support the credit market in the UK on a commercial basis for larger transactions, it no longer has any UK local partners who could handle transactions below €25 million.
www.eib.org

#Bodies

European Investment Fund (EIF)

Part of the European Investment Bank group, a specialist provider of risk finance to benefit small and medium-sized enterprises (SME) across Europe. Its shareholders are the European Investment Bank (EIB), the European Union, represented by the European Commission, and a wide range of public and private banks and financial institutions.

The EIF provides guarantees and credit enhancement to promote SME lending. Through its Structured Finance programme, it can facilitate the placement of debt with third party investors by guaranteeing the timely payment of debt's interest and principal. It can also share the risk on new leasing, in exchange for a fee, under its COSME Loan Guarantee Facility (formerly the Risk Sharing Instrument).

With EU support, the EIF provides uncapped guarantees to leasing companies on 50% of each eligible lease, potentially enabling lessors to offer finance for riskier asset classes or clients.

The EIF no longer operates in the UK, where the British Business Bank provides support of this nature.
www.eif.org

#Bodies

Evergreen lease

A lease agreement that extends automatically for fixed periods until notice is given by the lessee to cancel it. Although there are circumstances where it may be a valid technique, there is a risk that the agreement will not suit the needs of lessees if they are not fully aware of how the terms, including their rights to terminate.

#Contracts

Export leasing

When a manufacturer offers leasing options to customers in other countries. It could offer leases itself as a captive lessor working on a cross-border basis, set up captive lessor operations in the destination countries, partner with lessors in the destination countries, or partner with one or more lessors that works on an international basis.

#Market

Extension rental

Where a lease automatically continues beyond the initial term (or contains an option for the lessee to extend the rental period beyond the initial term), the amount of rentals that will be charged during that extension may simply be the same as the rentals during the initial term or the rentals could be lower or even peppercorn amounts.

#Contracts

F

Facility letter

A document that sets out a commitment for the lessor to finance equipment subject to conditions such as security, timescale and payment of any fees. Most likely to be relevant to big-ticket leases.

#Legal

Factoring

A form of asset-based finance, loans that are secured against specific trade receivables. Factoring firms ('factors') often provide 70% to 85% of the value of invoices up-front. They take on debt management and collecting responsibilities. When the invoices are paid, the factoring company makes the remaining balance available to their client less their fees.

#Alternatives

Fair value

The price that a well-informed buyer would pay for an asset in a competitive market. It has various uses in asset finance.

When underwriting a lease agreement, the lessor will want to know that the equipment price agreed between the potential lessee and the equipment supplier reflects the fair value.

For lease accounting, fair value is the amount for which an asset could be sold in an arm's length transaction, with neither buyer nor seller under any compulsion to buy or to sell.

A fair value purchase option is where, in a hire purchase arrangement, the lessee has the option to acquire the asset at its market value at the time that the option is exercised.

A fair renewal value is an extension rental that is calculated based on the then current fair market value.

#Accounting #Contracts

Fees

Any extra amounts charged by the lessor over and above the lease rentals. Firms may variously charge documentation, annual, insurance, renewal or other fees.

For regulated credit, any such fees should be included in the Annualised Percentage Rate and explained to the lessee before the lease is agreed. A firm must not impose charges on customers in default or arrears difficulties unless the charges are no higher than necessary to cover the reasonable costs of the firm.

#Contacts #Conduct

Fiduciary

A term indicating a level of trust between a customer as a potential lessee or borrower and an intermediary felt to be acting on their behalf. Where such a relationship exists, the intermediary cannot accept payments from third parties without disclosing this to the customer.

#Conduct #Legal

Finance and Leasing Association (FLA)

Founded in 1992 with the merger of the Finance Houses Association and the Equipment Leasing Association. It is split into three divisions, representing consumer finance, motor finance and asset finance. The Association is principally a representative body for the consumer finance and leasing industries. It operates codes of conduct for its consumer and business lenders, reviews complaints received about its members, and organises training, seminars and drinks receptions. Its Annual Dinner, held in February at the Grosvenor House Hotel, is one of the largest industry events of the year.
www.fla.org.uk

#Associations

Finance house

Traditionally, a non-bank finance company which funded consumer hire purchase agreements. More recently, any finance company specialising in hire purchase for both consumer and small business customers. The term is sometimes used interchangeably with 'lessor'.

#Market

Finance Houses Association

The former trade association for the instalment credit industry, its members provided hire purchase agreements mainly to consumers and smaller businesses. Founded in 1945, it merged with the Equipment Leasing Association in 1992 to form the Finance and Leasing Association. It established and ran the Finance Houses Diploma.

#Associations

Finance House Base Rate

An index that was maintained by the Finance and Leasing Association (FLA) until 2020. The rate was calculated at the end of each month by averaging the cost of three-month money in the interbank market ("LIBOR") over the previous eight weeks. The resulting figure was then rounded up to the next half point. The FLA stated that the process was entirely arithmetical and contained no discretionary element.

The index was used by some finance companies as a basis of calculating lending charges for mainly consumer agreements that are based on variable interest rates. It was not in common use in the business asset finance market. Most leasing agreements in the UK are fixed rate and where they are variable, they now tend to be based on the Bank of England base rate

#Market

Finance Houses Diploma

The Finance Houses Association's, and later the Finance and Leasing Association's, courses and qualifications. Many of today's leaders of the industry hold the qualification. It was discontinued around 2001 due to falling registrations. In 2018 the FLA replaced it with the London Institute of Banking and Finance's Diploma in Asset Finance (DipAF), see Diploma in Asset Finance.
www.libf.ac.uk/

#Operations

Finance lease

For lease accounting under IAS 17 of UK accounting rules until 2026, a lease that transfers substantially all of the 'risks and rewards' of ownership of an asset from the lessor to the lessee. This typically applies, for example, if ownership of the asset will transfer at the end of the lease, if there is a bargain purchase option, or if the lease can be extended at a rate below the market level. Other factors used to identify a finance lease include the length of the lease term compared to the economic life of the asset and the value of the minimum lease payments compared to the value of the asset.

Under IAS 17 finance leases are reported on the balance sheet of the lessee. Under IFRS 16, and UK financial reporting standards from 2026, operating leases will also be reported in a similar way, removing the distinction between the two types for lessee accounting.

Also known as a capital lease, especially in the US.

#Accounting #Products

Financial Accounting Standards Board (FASB)

The body that establishes financial accounting and reporting standards for use by US companies. In 2016, the FASB issued its new lease accounting rules in its Update No. 2016-02, Leases (Topic 842). Although developed alongside the International Accounting Standards Board's IFRS 16, the FASB rules still differentiate between operating and finance leases. Both types lead to a 'right-of-use' asset on the lessee's balance sheet, but the calculation and recognition of lease expenses vary. For finance leases, lessees report separately the asset depreciation from the finance costs (amortisation of the lease liability). For operating leases, lessees report only a single, total expense.
www.fasb.org

#Accounting

Financial Conduct Authority (FCA)

One of the regulators of the UK's financial services industry, working alongside the Prudential Regulatory Authority (PRA) and the Bank of England.

Financial services firms must be authorised by the FCA. They are listed on the FCA's Register, must follow the relevant parts of the FCA's Handbook of rules covering how they conduct their business, and report on their activities using the FCA's Gabriel system.

The most direct impact for lessors is on their conduct of business of regulated consumer credit agreements, but the FCA's Principles for Business apply across all activities of authorised firms. The Principles include the need to conduct business with integrity, due skill, care and diligence.
www.fca.org.uk

#Bodies #Conduct

Financial Intermediary & Broker Association (FIBA)

Trade association representing commercial finance brokers (who may also deal in asset finance) alongside bridging loan professionals, residential mortgage brokers, and independent financial advisers.
www.fiba.org.uk

#Associations

Financial Ombudsman Service (FOS)

Independent body with statutory powers to help settle individual disputes between consumers or small businesses and finance companies. It is paid for by the Financial Services industry through a levy on FCA-regulated firms.

Since 2014 'micro-enterprises' with fewer than ten employees can bring complaints about FCA-regulated firms to the FOS. About 99% of UK small businesses qualify. The complaint must first have been considered through the relevant firm's own complaints procedure and have received the final response from that firm.

Regulated firms pay a flat rate of £650 for each complaint investigated by the FOS after the first three complaints, in addition to the annual levy. Lessors dealing with regulated customers must inform customers they will have the option of using the FOS as part of the complaints handling process.
www.financial-ombudsman.org.uk

#Bodies #Conduct

Financial Reporting Advisory Board (FRAB)

Independent body established by HM Treasury to advise Government on financial reporting. In recent years, the FRAB has considered the application of IFRS 16 to public sector accounting rules, including the Government Financial Reporting Manual that is used by central government departments, the Department of Health and Social Care Group Accounting Manual that is used by the NHS, and the Code of Practice on Local Authority Accounting in the United Kingdom. IFRS 16 was applied to central government and NHS reporting from 2022, and to local authority reporting from 2024.

#Accounting #Public sector

Financial Reporting Council (FRC)

Body that develops and enforces financial reporting standards in the UK, it incorporates the former Accounting Standards Board. Expected to be replaced by a new body, the Audit, Reporting and Governance Authority.
www.frc.org.uk

#Accounting

Financial Reporting Standards (FRS)

The UK accounting rules followed by all companies other than those using international financial reporting standards. The key standard is FRS 102 which consolidated more than 70 topic-specific standards including the former leases standard SSAP 21. Small companies may be eligible to follow special rules for smaller firms that are included in a section of FRS 102, or the separate micro-entities standard FRS 105.

Before SSAP 21 was withdrawn, accountants in the industry used accompanying guidance that had been issued by the Finance and Leasing Association in 2000. The Statement of Recommended Practice (SORP) 'Accounting issues in the asset finance and leasing industry' was endorsed by the Accounting Standards Board and its parent the Financial Reporting Council (FRC). The SORP was withdrawn by the FRC when FRS 102 took effect but still provides useful insights into how to apply the lease accounting rules.

In March 2024, the FRC confirmed that UK accounting standards will change to follow IFRS 16 lease accounting rules, with minor adaptations, for reporting from 2026.

#Accounting

Fintech

Financial technology (or 'Fintech') companies rely on technology to deliver financial services that traditionally involve human effort.

The term is often associated with radical innovation which has the potential to disrupt existing business models in financial markets.

Although most lessors have been through a period of digital transformation (or 'digitisation'), so that most communications and records are now online, leasing remains an industry where humans have a key role. A 'pure' fintech firm might seek to make the interface with customers entirely online, or 'embedded' in the asset ordering process. See Embedded finance.

#Market

Fit out finance

Finance for fixtures, fittings and equipment that turn a building into a functioning workspace, such as a hotel or a gym.

Whilst typically associated with new-builds or full premise refurbishments, it can also apply to minor refurbishments or upgrades to business premises. It recognises the project nature of the investment, so rather than being restricted to DIMS assets, lenders will typically roll in significant elements of soft cost and fixtures. A prime example being the front-of-house carpet in a hotel, which has no recovery value but is a key asset to the hotel in the first impression it provides to guests.

#Assets #Products

Fittings

Items in buildings that are free standing or hung by screws, nails or hooks. Commercial leases will stipulate that any fittings added by the tenant must be removed at the end of the tenancy.

For tax purposes, they are generally categorised as Plant and machinery and are therefore eligible for capital allowances. However some may be categorised as Fixtures, if they are attached or fixed to the building in a more permanent way and may not then be eligible for capital allowances. HMRC provides detailed guidance on the correct categorisation. See Fit out finance

#Assets #Tax

Fixed assets

Items of plant, property and equipment used by a business for more than one accounting period (i.e. typically one year) and recognised on the user's balance sheet. They may be used for the purposes of production, the supply of goods or services, rental to others, or administration.

#Accounting

Fixed charge

A A form of security that secures obligations owed to the charge-holder (such as monies due to the charge-holder). It gives the charge-holder certain rights over a particular asset or assets that are subject to the fixed charge, and which is capable of charging both existing and future assets, (including the sales proceeds of such charged assets).

A fixed charge is not ownership of an asset but an 'encumbrance' over such asset. If a lessor is the legal owner of an asset that is leased to a lessee, the lessor cannot charge the asset but the lessor might require additional security by way of a fixed charge against a different asset (which may be owned by the lessee or a third party) perhaps in circumstances where the asset being leased has limited resale value.

A fixed charge has the advantage of ranking before a floating charge in the order of repayment on an insolvency, however, it is important that the charge-holder has sufficient control over the charged assets under a fixed charge otherwise there is a risk that the fixed charge could be challenged and recategorized as a floating charge.

#Legal

Fixed rate

A lease where the lease payments do not fluctuate with changes in interest rates. Most lease agreements with smaller businesses are on fixed rates (although there may be a clause allowing upward adjustments if UK tax rates increase).

#Contracts

Fixed term rental

A lease where the asset is expected to be returned to the lessor at the end of the lease period without a contractual option to extend that period. That does not prevent the lessor and lessee from negotiating further rentals over a defined additional rental period or selling the assets (which was the subject of the lease) to the former lessee at a Fair value. Fixed term rental tends to be used in support of vendor programmes, as the vendors' aim would be to replace old assets for new.

#Products

Fixtures

Assets that become an integral part of the buildings in which they are installed.

If classified as fixtures, leased assets may be difficult to remove and, therefore, provide little or no security. A landlord's waiver might be required to facilitate removal.

For accounting, an agreement for leasing an asset that is a fixture would almost certainly be classified as a finance rather than operating lease.

For tax purposes, a fixture would normally not be classified as Plant and Machinery, and so would not be eligible for capital allowances. HMRC provides guidance on 'integral fixtures' that would qualify for capital allowances, including for example escalators and external solar heating.

#Accounting #Assets #Tax

FLA Checklist

Under guidance linked to the FLA's Business Finance Code, members have the option to provide a checklist published by the FLA to customers 'when the value of the assets financed is less than £100k or when it is appropriate to provide the checklist'. The checklist provides 12 recommendations to lessees that are intended to help them to make successful use of asset finance.

#Contracts

Flat rate

The interest charge for a lease, calculated by dividing the total interest over the contract by the number of years, then dividing the result by the amount financed x 100 to provide a percentage.

The alternative, which is less commonly used, is a reducing balance rate, where the interest charged is divided by the outstanding net book value of the lease in each year.

#Finance

Fleet

The company car and van fleet market is one of the largest segments of the UK leasing industry. More than half of all new cars sold in the UK are purchased for the fleet market. The largest fleet lessors, according to the Asset Finance 50, are Ayvens (including Leaseplan and ALD) owned by Societe Generale, Lex owned by Lloyds Bank, Alphabet owned by BMW, and Arval owned by BNP Paribas.

#Market

Floating charge

A charge over all the assets of a company, or a class of those assets, rather than a fixed charge over a specific asset or assets. The company granting a charge over those assets will typically continue its business in the ordinary way in relation to the charged assets (including disposing of such assets) without the need to obtain the consent of the charge-holder A floating charge ranks after a Fixed charge in the order of repayment on an insolvency.

#Legal #Risk

Forbearance

The toleration of late payments or other contractual breaches. Under FCA rules, firms are required to treat regulated customers in default or in arrears with forbearance and due consideration. Examples of forbearance include allowing deferment of payments, suspending interest or allowing token payments to be made for a period of time.

Although the need for forbearance in regulated asset finance contracts is rare, many firms were required to provide forbearance (such as payment holidays) to business customers during the Covid pandemic.

#Conduct

Foreign Account Tax Compliance Act (FATCA)

The United States' Foreign Account Tax Compliance Act (FATCA), requires that foreign financial Institutions and certain other bodies report to the US Government on the foreign assets held by their US account holders. It means that if a US business has leased assets in the UK, details might need to be reported unless various exemptions and exclusions apply. Captive finance companies are excluded. Reporting is bi-annual, online via HM Revenue and Customs.

#Tax

Fraud

Intentional misrepresentation, concealment or other deceit to the detriment of another person.

Lessors are at risk from many types of fraud. Risk officers might say there is nothing new under the sun in asset finance fraud. The risk of fraud can be mitigated greatly but there is always a trade-off between attempting to completely remove risk and keeping down the costs of providing a good customer service. Most fraud originates from customers or from intermediaries and suppliers and sometimes collusion between them.

Customer fraud is often in the form of false information in finance applications, doctored bank statements or falsified company balance sheets for example. Such risks can be mitigated through identity and address verification, obtaining credit references, CIFAS and Dun & Bradstreet Critical Intelligence System checks, the use of open-banking systems, asset inspections, asset valuation checks, and procedures to sense-check equipment requirements against the profile of the applicant's business.

Fraud by broker or vendor intermediaries can be difficult to identify, particularly if the customer is complicit. Mitigants include appraisal of new intermediaries, on-site reviews of existing intermediaries, controls on payouts including confirming bank account details, and only paying direct to the appropriate parties once the equipment is confirmed as satisfactorily delivered.

Like any business, a lessor is also subject to the risk of internal fraud by its own staff or contractors. Mitigants include requiring multiple sign-offs for large transactions and segregation of duties.

In recent years some of the largest frauds suffered by the industry have been caused by multi financing fraud (where the same asset is funded by more than one lessor) or comfort / side-letters.

#Risk

Fresh air fraud

Where a lessor pays out for goods that do not exist or have not been delivered, leaving the lessor with no security. The lessor is likely to have been presented with false invoices, so instead of financing assets they are left financing only 'fresh air'. As the lessee is likely to be party to the fraud, confirmation of receipt of the goods is insufficient. The risk is mitigated through underwriting checks on all parties involved: customer, supplier and any intermediary. See Multi-financing.

#Risk

Full payout lease

A lease where the agreed lease payments in the initial lease term are sufficient to pay for the asset, interest, other costs and the margin for the lessor. When pricing a full-payout lease the lessor does not rely on the asset having residual value or on there being a secondary period.

#Products

Full service lease

Lease where the lessor provides maintenance, repair and insurance. More frequently referred to as Contract hire.

#Products

Funder

Another name for a lessor or lender. If there is one or more intermediate lessor/s (for example where there is both a head-lease and sub-lease), the underlying funder is the head-lessor.

#Market

Funding

How a lessor raises cash for leasing assets. The options include use of deposits for a bank, using own equity, or borrowing the funds to lend. Borrowing options include Block discounting, issuing Commercial paper, Securitisation, or use of relevant British Business Bank schemes.

#Funding

G

General Data Protection Regulation (GDPR)

The European data protection laws that took effect in the UK in May 2018 by way of the Data Protection Act 2018. For lessors and intermediaries, the rules (aimed at providing more protection for individuals) are generally consistent with the tone of those in the pre-existing UK data protection legislation, but (like so much regulation facing lessors) now with tighter compliance rules, including enhanced obligations concerning record keeping.

GDPR impacts business leasing in so far as firms hold data that identifies living individuals. It requires firms to issue privacy notices to customers, protect the data they hold from loss or misuse, and in relevant circumstances, to enable individuals to access their data and to have it corrected or erased.

The rules have been quite problematic for introducers, as they must not only issue their own privacy information but often also that of the funders. The Information Commissioner's Office has agreed with The NACFB and the FLA that intermediaries may provide website links to privacy policies of funders, rather than maintain stocks of each firm's paperwork.

#Regulation

Gross interest margin

The difference between the interest paid on the lessors borrowed funds and the interest charged to the lessee. Sometimes referred to as the Interest rate spread.

#Funding

Gross investment in the lease

For lease accounting, the sum of the lease payments that the lessee will pay the lessor under a finance lease, together with the expected residual value of the asset.

#Accounting

Growth Guarantee Scheme (GGS)

Launched in 2024 as the successor to the Recovery Loan Scheme, aims to support access to growing small businesses (those with turnover of up to £45m). The Scheme, operated by the British Business Bank, provides lender with a 70% government-backed guarantee for defaults. It is available through asset finance lenders, alongside other types of business finance.

The lender must consider that the borrower has a viable business proposition, and the borrower must not be a business in financial difficulty.

Market

Guarantee

A promise made by the guarantor to the lender to: (i) repay debt that is owed by a borrower to the lender in circumstances where the borrower fails to perform its payment obligations to the lender; and / or (ii) perform any other type of specific obligation, in the event of the default of another person primarily responsible for it. See also Personal guarantee.

#Contracts

Guild of Business Finance Professionals

An unincorporated not for profit association set up in 2024 by a founding group of leasing and asset finance brokers, to act as a collective voice for qualifying individuals working towards higher ethical standards in the corporate lending sector.
www.bfpguild.org

#Credit

H

Hard assets

A term used by lessors to refer to assets that meet the DIMS (Durable, Identifiable, Moveable and Saleable) criteria. Assets are generally classified as either hard or soft, but there may be many different views on how to draw a line between the two types.

#Assets

Head lessor

The lessor that owns the asset and leases it to one or a series of intermediate lessors, which may then lease it on (under a sub-lease) to a customer (as sub-lessee) on either a disclosed or undisclosed basis.

#Legal #Market

Healthcare Financial Management Association

Professional body for finance staff working in UK hospital trusts and the wider healthcare industry. It provides technical briefings to many NHS finance directors including on lease accounting rules and their application to the NHS.
www.hfma.org.uk

#Public sector

Hell or high water

Standard term in a lease agreement that confirms the unconditional obligation of the lessee to pay rents for any equipment element for the duration of the agreement, regardless of any event affecting wider aspects of the overall agreement, for example problems with the asset, the failure of a maintenance provider to perform maintenance services or acts of nature.

#Contracts

High net worth

For consumer credit regulation, an exemption that may apply where the customer earns more than £150,000 and/or has net assets excluding their main residence of more than £500,000. Outside consumer credit regulation, the term is also used more generally by lessors to refer to wealthy customers.

#Conduct

High value leases

See Big-ticket.

#Market

Hire

Under consumer credit law, a hire or lease agreement is where the lessee has no option to buy the asset from the lessor at the end of the term. If there is any purchase option, whether it is written into the hire or lease agreement or offered separately, it is a credit and not a hire or lease agreement. See also Lease.

#Legal #Conduct

Hire purchase

An arrangement that gives the lessee an option to buy the asset from the lessor at the end of the lease period, provided the lessee has kept to the terms of the agreement. Hire purchase accounts for around 50% of the UK leasing market by value.

Although there is not an obligation to take up the option to purchase, there is often a Bargain purchase option, so it is regarded as likely to be exercised.

For tax an agreement is only treated as hire purchase if there is a bargain purchase option. For consumer credit hire purchase is a form of credit and not hire, regardless of the cost of the purchase option. See also Lease Purchase.

#Products #Tax

HM Revenue and Customs (HMRC)

The UK tax authority, responsible for the administration and collection of tax including corporation tax. Its internal manual, Business Leasing, is published on the www.gov.uk website. The manual is intended to provide HMRC personnel with an introduction to lease accounting and lease accounting taxation, with special emphasis on the leasing of plant or machinery. The size of the manual leaves no doubt about the complexity of the UK's lease taxation rules.

#Bodies #Tax

HM Treasury (HMT)

Government department that sets economic and financial policy, including the tax, financial conduct and prudential rules which are implemented by HM Revenue and Customs, the Financial Conduct Authority and the Prudential Regulation Authority. Oversees public spending, including capital spending across Government departments and initiatives including the British Business Bank's schemes.

#Bodies

Holdback

Where the lessor retains part of the cost price of the asset until the end of the lease agreement, rather than paying it all at the outset. This method can be used to support an arrangement where the lessor agrees to loosen its usual criteria for lessee eligibility, to support the supplier's sales. The amounts retained form a loss pool to cover the extra risk if this is realised. Also referred to as retention.

#Contracts #Risk

Holdover

Where the lease terms allow the contract to automatically roll over into a fixed-period extension where the customer has not notified the lessor that they intend to return the asset at the end of the initial term.

The FLA Business Fnance Code effectively bans the practice. The Code requires lessors to give the customer the right to terminate the agreement at any time by giving not more than 3 months' notice when a business finance agreement is continued without amendment beyond a minimum/initial period of hire.

#Contracts

Holiday

Where a lessor permits a lessee to not pay a certain number of lease payments. The missed lease payments, with additional interest, may be added to the end of the lease agreement. Alternatively, the remaining lease payments may be adjusted upwards.

#Contracts

HPI

Supplier of data solutions to the car market, including a register that lessors can use to show their ownership of leased assets. See Asset registration.

#Assets

Hurdle rate

The minimum required rate of return for an investment project in a discounted cash flow analysis. If the cost of a project is too high, possibly due to the interest rate inherent in the lease, then it may fall short of the hurdle rate. A lower rate should, therefore, result in more investment taking place, everything else being equal.

#Finance

I

IAS 17

The former international accounting standard for leases, replaced by IFRS 16 for reporting periods ending from January 2019. First published in 1982, it was effective from 1984 and was revised in 2003.

#Accounting

IFRS 9

The international accounting standard for financial instruments that took effect in January 2018. It sets the rules for how banks and other financial institutions should measure financial assets and liabilities.

The key relevance to leasing, as compared to the previous rules under IAS 39, is the tighter impairment rules that determine how contacts that might fall into default or loss should be reported. Under the new "expected loss" model, firms must now report based on the forecast risk of defaults, rather than (only) historical trends.

Under IFRS 9, the lease portfolio should be separated into 3 parts: Agreements in Stage 1 are 'performing'' (being paid on time). Stage 2 agreements are 'underperforming', likely to show some late payment or other signs of distress, but with the potential to recover 'performing'. Stage 3 agreements are credit-impaired, where the lessor does not expect a full recovery. The lessor will apply an Impairment provision separately to each part of the portfolio. For most leasing firms the effect of the change on the accounts is limited, as the probability of future losses is likely to be aligned with historic levels. However, the evidence needed to support the forecasts is more substantial, requiring analysis of both internal and external (e.g. general economic) factors. This aligns accounting with prudential regulation, as firms using the Advanced Internal Ratings Based method will already have models based on a similar approach.

For non-banks or banks using the Standardised approach for prudential regulation, the extra data and analysis involved can be substantial. Some may take the view that it is most efficient to treat leasing as part of a wider portfolio of SME lending. However, for firms able to collect sufficient leasing-specific data, IFRS 9 may help to demonstrate the lower risk advantages of leasing compared to other forms of lending.

#Accounting

IFRS 15

The international accounting standard for revenue recognition that took effect in January 2018. Revenue should be recognised when a 'performance obligation' is satisfied by transferring a promised good or service to a customer.

It has limited impact on lessors, as IFRS 16 determines the revenue recognition for lease contracts. It may impact reporting of non-lease revenue, for example maintenance or other services connected to leases.

#Accounting

IFRS 16

The international accounting standard for leases, published in January 2016 and effective from January 2019. It is the outcome of the IASB's project to improve lease accounting started in 2006.

For the lessee, IFRS 16 removed the distinction between operating leases and finance leases. Instead there is only a single type of lease, the 'right of use' lease, which will be reported as an asset on the lessee's balance sheet.

The IASB decided that changing lessor accounting was unnecessary. Lessors still report operating lease assets on their own balance sheets using rules very like IAS 17.

The 'right of use' model is controversial. Businesses that lease identical or similar assets may report very different asset values depending on the lease terms, and both the lessee and the lessor will report an asset on their balance sheets, which some see as double counting.

#Accounting

Impairment

For agreements where the lessor assesses there is a risk of not being paid in full by the lessee, the agreement is identified as 'impaired'. For financial accounting purposes, the lessor will estimate the expected loss from impairment across its portfolio. This estimate, the impairment provision, reduces the book value of the portfolio in the accounts and the company's accounting profit.

If the lessor has made a reasonable estimate of future losses, as individual write-offs occur, they have no impact on profitability, as it is only the movement in the impairments balance that impacts the profit and loss (income) statement.

A typical level of impairments balances in the industry is between 0.5% and 1.0% of gross book, although the level varies according to the risk appetite of the lessor, it success in managing risk, and the overall economic environment.

#Accounting #Risk

Implicit lease rate

For lease accounting, the interest rate that when applied to the agreed lease payments at the start of the agreement will discount those payments to the cost of the equipment leased less any expected residual value. May also be referred to as the 'rate implicit in the lease' or the 'effective interest rate'.

#Accounting

In-life functions

Activities involved in managing existing lease agreements, including any required asset, contract, customer or supplier management.

#Operations

Indemnity

An undertaking by one person to meet the liability of another. Lessors will generally include indemnity provisions in the lease agreement under which the lessee accepts responsibility for all risks associated with the asset during the term of the lease agreement.

For example, the lessee may agree to pay any losses, claims, actions and legal expenses that may arise or be incurred by the lessor if someone is injured when using the asset. A company director, holding company or subsidiary may also indemnify the lessor in relation to any amounts owed by the lessee; this often forms part of a guarantee.

#Legal

Independent lessor

The term is used in two main ways. First, as referring to a lessor that is not a 'captive', that is, independent of a manufacturer or supplier and so is free to offer finance on any asset. Second, and more commonly in the UK, as referring to a lessor that is neither a captive nor a bank-owned leasing company.

#Market

Information Commissioner's Office (ICO)

The UK's regulator of information rights, including Data Protection and freedom of information. Lessors and brokers need to register as data controllers with the ICO. Sharing of data on individuals with credit reference agencies and for fraud avoidance purposes should follow ICO guidelines. The ICO has played a major role in the recent introduction of the European General Data Protection Regulations into the UK through the Data Protection Act 2018.
www.ico.org.uk

#Regulation

Initial direct costs

In lease accounting, the costs of obtaining a lease that would not otherwise be incurred. For the lessee, they might include delivery or installation. For the lessor, they might include broker commissions.

#Accounting

Insolvency

The inability of a company to meet its debts as they become due. An insolvent business can be placed into administration or wound up. Administration allows for the reorganisation of the company with a moratorium placed over existing debts. A winding up is done using either a creditors' voluntary liquidation or a compulsory liquidation. It leads to the dissolution of the company. See also Administration order.

#Legal #Risk

Insolvency Practitioner (IP)

An individual who is licensed and authorised to act in relation to a party facing insolvency, be it an individual, partnership or company. They assess that party's current financial standing, the extent of their indebtedness to various creditors and their ability to repay the debt. They often have the authority to dispose of certain Assets to mitigate the party's overall indebtedness.

In carrying out their duties, IPs must decide at what stage to contact any lessors with interests in a case. They may contact a lessor at an early stage if they are confident they can easily reach a designated individual who has experience in dealing with insolvencies and can be expected to cooperate with the IP's efforts to maintain the business as a going concern.

#Risk

Inspection

Asset inspections are often undertaken to verify the existence and confirm the location and condition of assets, as a tool for discovering fraud and mitigating the risk of fraud. Lease agreements will often include inspection provisions. Various options are available in the market, including the lessor using their own staff, asking a broker to inspect, or using a third-party inspection service.

#Assets #Risk

Instalment credit

Form of credit where the borrower repays the loan over time, typically in equal instalments. The loan may be for the purpose of buying an asset, in which case the borrower owns the asset from the outset, so it is not a lease for accounting purposes but may still be considered to be Asset finance.

#Alternatives

Institutional investors

Financial services firms that invest money on behalf of individuals or businesses. Includes pension funds, insurance companies, unit and investment trusts, and venture capitalists. In the US, institutional investors are a major source of funding for the leasing industry, and their role is slowly but steadily growing in the UK with more asset finance firms starting to issue Asset backed securities.

#Funding

Insurance

The lessee will usually be required to insure leased assets. The insurance should generally cover the replacement value of the asset against a range of defined risks, including fire, theft and damage and third party liability. The lessor will usually be entitled to ask to see the policy.

If the lessee does not show that a suitable policy is in place the contract may permit the lessor to add the cost of insurance to the lessee's payments. In that case, the insured party is then typically the lessor rather than lessee.

#Contracts

Intangible asset

A non-physical asset, such as licences, software, brand names and trademarks. It can be difficult for lessors to lease intangible assets as the nature of the asset means they can provide limited or no security, so a loan may be more appropriate, however specialised lessors can often overcome such obstacles.

#Assets

Interest

The price of money over time, e.g. the contract period for an asset finance agreement. Lessors pay interest for their borrowed funds and charge interest on their leases.

The difference between the interest paid on the lessors borrowed funds and the interest charged to the lessee is the Gross interest margin.

#Finance #Funding

Interest free

See Zero percent finance, and Subsidy.

#Market

Interest rate risk

Risk that arises from changing interest rates. For a lessor, it is principally the risk that having lent at one rate, it will need to raise funds at a higher rate during the term of the agreement. To mitigate the risk, lessors can borrow for terms equivalent to their lending, or hedge against changes to rates. For a lessee, it is the risk that rates may increase, which is mitigated by agreeing a fixed rate contract.

#Funding #Risk

Interest rate spread

See Gross interest margin.

#Funding

Internal financing

Where a firm purchases an asset using funds produced from its own operations, rather than external financing such as leasing.

#Alternatives

International Finance and Leasing Association (IFLA)

An association of leasing companies from around the world. It aims to be a platform for sharing industry information and best practices. It does not intend to be a representative body. There is a limit of one company per country and in 2024 there were 15 members, mostly from Europe with the UK member being Allied Irish Bank. The US is represented by the Equipment Leasing and Finance Association rather than by a company. The IFLA has its own song, sung to Andrew Lloyd Webber's "Amigos Para Siempre" ("Friends for Life"). *www.ifla.com*

#Associations

International leasing

An agreement where the asset is located in a different country to where the agreement is transacted. This leads to a wide range of extra considerations for lessors covering areas such as legal rights, tax, foreign exchange risk and social and political risk. Most international leasing takes place out of countries with the lowest corporate tax rates, including Ireland for the aviation sector.

#Market

Internet of Things (IoT)

The use of networking components, including sensors and transmitters, placed in assets to transmit data about that asset and how it is working. Sensors in many commercial and agricultural vehicles, for example, help optimise the efficiency both of the vehicle and of the job it is being used for.

The IoT makes leasing more complex as many assets now comprise a combination of the core equipment together with networking equipment and software applications. The equipment is also likely to have a longer useful life than the IoT technology.

#Business

Introducer Appointed Representative (IAR)

For the FCA regulation of consumer credit, an Appointed Representative who is limited to effecting introductions, including providing customer's contact details to an authorised firm and distributing promotional material. An IAR should not discuss finance options with their customer.

#Intermediaries #Conduct

Invoice discounting

A type of factoring where the factor lends money to the firm, but the firm continues to collect the money itself rather than having the factor do this.

#Alternatives

Invoice fraud

Where an inaccurate invoice is provided by a supplier or the supplier's invoice is altered in an attempt to defraud the lessor. There are many possible variations. The value of the asset and the deposit paid might be altered to make it appear the lessee has paid a larger deposit than in reality. The supplier might issue an invoice for new equipment when used equipment has been supplied.

#Risk

J

Joint Money Laundering Steering Group (JMLSG)

A working group made up of the UK's financial services trade associations, the JMLSG publishes guidance on how to interpret and apply the UK money laundering regulations. It includes a chapter dealing with leases which was updated in May 2018. The chapter identifies features of asset finance that can increase or decrease the risk of money-laundering or terrorist funding. These include:

- Paying lease rentals over a medium-term period provides a very slow means of 'layering' (using transactions to make it difficult to trace an illegal source of cash) the proceeds of crime *(a feature suggesting low risk)*
- The amount of asset finance obtainable is generally limited by the financial situation of the customer, limiting the possibility of layering a lot of money to financially stronger businesses *(low risk)*
- Customers must acquire business assets, which may be soft assets with low resale value *(low risk)*, hard assets with reliable resale value *(medium risk)*, or be luxury assets that might be desirable to criminals in their own right such as luxury cars *(high risk)*
- The lessor usually pays the supplier of the goods directly *(low risk)* but sometimes may pay the customer *(medium risk)*
- Rental payments are generally paid by direct debit from a UK bank account *(low risk)* but might be paid by cash *(high risk)*
- Any overpayments will generally be reimbursed to the business named on the agreement *(low risk)* but might be requested to be paid to a third party *(high risk)*

The guidance suggests that lessors should assess:

- The suitability of the asset for the customer
- The credentials of the vendor of the asset.
- For sale and leaseback contracts, the original invoices and the credentials of the supplier of assets
- The reasons for an unusually early termination of a lease agreement, as this could be a sign of layering.

Overall, the JMLSG notes that the features of asset finance make it a 'low risk' of money laundering or terrorist financing, providing sensible credit policies and procedures are followed based on the above features.

Firms regulated by the Financial Conduct Authority must follow the FCA's handbook, including its Financial Crime Guide. Firms may not rely only on the JMLSG guidance to ensure compliance with the FCA handbook or the underlying legal obligations. The FCA has confirmed it will consider the JMLSG guidance when deciding whether a firm has breached the regulations, although it is not legally obliged to do so.
www.jmlsg.org.uk

#Bodies #Regulation #Risk

K

Kickback

An unlawful practice under the Bribery Act 2010, whereby an illegal payment is made intended as compensation for preferential treatment or any other type of improper service received.

For example, an equipment supplier might incentivise a broker or a finance company representative to misrepresent a deal by knowingly submitting a false invoice to the lender and in return receive a cash payment from the supplier.

#Risk

Know Your Customer (KYC)

Due diligence checks that should take place in respect of a customer as part of a firm's anti-money laundering procedures. The Joint Money Laundering Steering Group guidance sets out suggested checks.

#Regulation

L

Landlord's waiver

An agreement between the lessor and the landlord of the lessee's business premises where the asset is to be kept. It allows the lessor to enter the premises to inspect and/or remove the assets. It usually provides that the landlord agrees not to take possession, claim any rights in, or create security or any other encumbrance over, the assets. It also waives any terms of the lessee's property lease that would classify the assets as fixtures of the building and prevent their removal by the lessor.

Landlords can be resistant to signing such waivers. If a lessor still wishes to proceed with a lease, they can seek to protect themselves by issuing a formal notification of the existence of the lease to the landlord after the event, which prevents a landlord claiming to be unaware of the lessor's ownership of an asset.

#Legal

Late payment interest

A higher rate of interest which may be applied to lease payments which have not been paid when they fell due under the terms of the lease contact. For regulated business, the FCA rulebook states that firms must not impose charges on customers in default or arrears difficulties unless the charges are no higher than necessary to cover the reasonable costs of the firm.

#Contracts #Credit

Lease

Agreement by which the owner of the asset (the 'lessor') allows another party (the 'lessee') to use an asset in return for payment. Some would use the term to refer specifically to hire agreements that have no purchase option, but a wider definition may also apply. See Leasing.

#Market

Lease payments

The amounts paid by the lessee to the lessor during the term of the lease agreement. May also be referred to as rentals, although lease payments may also include fees and other charges.

#Contracts

Lease purchase

A lease where title is expected to transfer to the lessee upon the lessee exercising their option to purchase the assets by paying an option to purchase fee at the end of the lease term.

The option to purchase fee may or may not be a nominal fee. If it is nominal (a bargain purchase option) it is a Hire purchase for tax purposes.

#Products

Lease rate factor

The regular lease payment amount as a percent of the total cost of the leased asset. It is a measure of limited use, since on its own it gives no reliable indication of the interest rate inherent in the lease. Salespeople often use a lease rate factor table to calculate a rental more quickly.

#Contracts

Lease term

The minimum period for which the lessee agrees to lease an asset from the lessor. Also referred to as the non-cancellable period, primary lease period or minimum term. For lease accounting, the lease term will vary from the minimum period if the lessee has an option to extend or terminate a lease and is reasonably certain to exercise that option.

The period for which the lessee agrees to lease an asset from the lessor. Also referred to as the non-cancellable period, Primary lease period, hire period, minimum term or period, or fixed term or period.

If the lease agreement is a minimum period lease or a lease with secondary rental, the lessee will have the option to extend the leasing of the asset beyond the expiry of the lease term. If the lease agreement is a fixed term rental, the leasing of the assets usually ends on expiry of the lease term, unless extended by agreement between the lessor and lessee.

For lease accounting, the lease term will vary from the minimum period if the lessee has an option to extend or terminate a lease and is reasonably certain to exercise that option.

#Accounting #Contracts

Lease vs. buy

The technique of comparing leasing and purchasing options by considering the cashflows, including the tax effects, and discounting them to present value. Rather than carry this out for every asset, many larger businesses develop and review a leasing policy on a regular basis. They consider factors including the availability and cost of cash, tax, and the wider advantages and possible disadvantages of leasing.

#Finance

Lease with sales agency

Lease agreement where at the end of the lease term the lessee is automatically appointed as the lessor's agent to dispose of the assets. The agent is usually entitled to a rebate of rentals equivalent to a major element of the net proceeds of sale.

#Products

Lease with secondary rental

Lease agreement where at the end of the lease term the lessee can continue to rent the assets for a nominal annual fee (the historic standard for small ticket leases is the equivalent of the previous monthly rental, but only annually). This preserves the hiring relationship and can continue for as long as the customer wishes to retain the assets. This type of agreement tends to be used with higher value assets e.g. trucks. It is a form of Full payout lease.

#Products

Leaseurope

The umbrella trade body representing the leasing and automotive rental industries in Europe. Its 42 national members in 2024 were the national trade associations across 31 countries in Europe. Founded in 1972 as the European Federation of Leasing Company Associations. UK member bodies are the FLA and BVRLA.

Based in Brussels, Leaseurope is governed by a Board of 12 heads of leasing firms that meets quarterly and by a General Assembly consisting of all member bodies that meets annually.

The Annual Convention, held each year over two days in October, is the largest gathering of senior leasing industry practitioners from across Europe.
www.leaseurope.org

#Associations

Leaseurope Index

Leaseurope's quarterly survey of European leasing and automotive rental companies. In addition to volumes and portfolios, the survey tracks cost/income, profitability, cost of risk, return on assets and return on equity ratios.
www.leaseurope.org

#Operations

Leasing

Leasing is not a term specifically defined in law. It is defined in accounting regulations, but not in other areas of regulation (that tend to cross-refer to the accounting regulation),

In law, a leasing contract is seen as a relationship of 'bailment', meaning there is a temporary transfer of assets from one person to another. Similarly, for accounting purposes under international accounting rules, a leasing contract gives the 'right of use' of an asset to another person.

So is any contract of 'bailment' in law, or one that provides the 'right of use' for accounting purposes, leasing? Generally, yes, but with certain refinements:

- In common use of the term 'leasing' it is usual to exclude short-term rentals from the definition of the leasing market. There is no clear line, but bailments of less than 12 months are generally considered to be part of the short-term rental

market rather than leases. Under the new international lease accounting standard, IFRS 16, lessees have the option not to report leases of less than 12 months on their balance sheets.
- It is common to focus on business, rather than individual consumer, leasing when discussing the leasing market, with the term 'hire' being more common in the consumer market. But this is changing, as leasing becomes more relevant to consumers as we move to a more sustainable, circular economy.

There are a host of different bailment arrangements in common use. Some include the word 'lease', others do not – such as hire purchase and conditional sale. For accounting and tax purposes, they are all likely to be categorised as leases.

The term 'asset finance' is often assumed to be synonymous with 'leasing'. However, it can also include asset-based loans, where there is no bailment, as the borrower owns the asset. Most asset finance agreements, however, are leases as asset-based loans remain relatively uncommon. See also Asset Finance, Hire.

#Market

Leasing-as-a service

The general concept of 'as-a-service' is an assumption that the traditional model of owning assets is outdated, and instead businesses want to be able to use assets without having to own them. In many respects, this is exactly what an operating lease is, so 'leasing-as-a-service' might seem to be nothing new.

However, the term can probably more usefully be seen to be describing a combination of short-term rental and longer-term operating leasing arrangements. Businesses want flexibility to pay for assets as they need them, but on a longer-term basis than a short term hire. Meanwhile the lessor might be able to move equipment between customers, making better (and more sustainable) use of assets.

This exposes lessors to the risk that assets are used less than they might have expected so it is difficult to deliver. A combination of partnerships with equipment manufacturers, and long-term partnerships with customers may be needed to deliver leasing-as-service profitably.

Despite the difficulties, this business model could be seen as creating new opportunities to serve the UK's largest companies, most of which currently make limited use of leasing.

#ESG #Products

Leasing Broker Federation

Membership organisation supporting car and van leasing brokers and small fleet operating companies. The Federation was launched in 2015 and is run by Business Car Manager Ltd. It has around 100 members.
www.leasingbrokernews.co.uk

#Associations

Leasing Foundation

UK-based body established in 2012, that aims to ensure that the leasing industry is as successful as possible and continues to play a vital role in helping organisations in the UK access the finance they need.

It has five key focus areas – innovation, young people, diversity & inclusion, sustainability and giving.

The Foundation's activities have included mental health awareness events, a programme to celebrate of International Women's Day, a future leadership programme, networking events for young individuals, charity fundraising events including a summer party, and sustainability and innovation workshops.
www.leasingfoundation.org

#Associations

Leasing Life

Trade publication owned by information solutions and technologies company Timetric, part of Global Data. The monthly magazine is focused on the UK but includes coverage of the wider European market. It covers equipment leasing and another Timetric publication Motor Finance covers car leasing. Runs an

annual European awards dinner.
www.leasinglife.com, www.motorfinanceonline.com

#Market

Leasing World

Independent trade publication founded in 2005. There is a printed magazine with a digital edition, and a news website. In 2012 launched Broker World, aimed at asset finance brokers. Runs an annual UK awards dinner. *www.leasingworld.co.uk, www.broker-world.com*

#Market

Lessee

User of an asset owned by someone else under the terms of a lease agreement. May also be referred to as a hirer.

#Contracts

Lessor

Owner of an asset used by someone else under the terms of a lease agreement. May also be referred to as an owner.

#Contracts

Leveraged lease

A lease agreement where the cost of the asset is, in effect, split between the lessor and a third-party lender. The legal owner of the asset is the lessor. The lessor offers the asset as security for a loan from the third-party lender. The lender has restricted recourse to the lessee and the asset being leased. Leveraged leases tend to be more common in the US.

#Funding

Lien

A right to retain assets owned by another party until that party has paid money that it owes. A lease agreement should normally prevent a lessee from creating a lien against a leased asset. An asset finance provider might use a lien against non-leased assets as security.

#Risk

Limited company

A privately-owned company, meaning that the shares are not traded on a stock market. A shareholder's liability is limited to the value of the shares that they own but have not paid for. Leasing to limited companies is outside of the scope of FCA regulation of consumer credit.

#Business

Limited Liability Partnership (LLP)

A business owned by its partners, each of whom shares responsibility for the business. An individual partner's liability is limited to the amount they invest in the business.

#Business

Line of credit

A flexible borrowing facility allowing the customer to borrow up to a maximum amount over a period of time. The mechanics of a line of credit can apply equally to leasing, e.g. a customer can be guaranteed lease facilities for a total value of assets. One of the benefits of leasing is that it helps businesses preserve their capacity to borrow if they are getting close to using up other lines of credit.

#Alternatives

Liquidation

The process of winding up a company. A liquidation can be arranged on either a voluntary or a compulsory basis. A voluntary liquidation can be a creditor's voluntary liquidation, where the owners choose to liquidate the business because it cannot pay its debts, or a members' voluntary liquidation, where the business can settle its remaining debts, but the owners wish to close it.

#Risk

Listed company

A public company listed on the London Stock Exchange, including the AIM for smaller growing companies, or another stock exchange. Listed companies are required to follow international accounting rules.

#Business

Loan to value ratio

Ratio of the amount lent or advance to the actual value of an asset being financed.

#Operations

Long funding lease

For corporation tax rules, a lease that is considered by HMRC to be a financing arrangement. It excludes hire purchase. Includes all finance leases longer than 7 years; a finance lease with term between 5 and 7 years meeting certain criteria including a low residual value; and an operating lease with term longer than 5 years meeting certain criteria including the term being more than 65% of the asset's useful life and/or the lease payments being more than 80% of the asset's original value.

The lessee claims the capital allowances for a long funding lease (as happens also for hire purchase) for and offsets the interest element of the lease payments against profits. The intention of these complicated rules was to align the tax treatment of longer leases with that of taking out a loan to buy the equipment.

#Tax

Loss Given Default (LGD)

Ratio of the loss due to the default of a borrower to the amount outstanding at default. The LGD for leasing is measured after any benefit obtained from selling the asset is realised. It is reported as a percentage of the exposure at default, being the difference between the cashflows received by the lessor and those contracted to be paid.

#Prudential

Lumia

Launched in 2023, following the Arena Television fraud case, a central register of borrowing for the UK asset finance industry. It aims to provides a clear insight into a customer's lending exposure as reported by lenders, to alert lenders to undisclosed or rapidly increasing borrowing and possible fraudulent activity (e.g. falsified balance sheets or multi financing).

A lessor might decide to conduct additional checks if the database suggests multiple lenders have exposures to a single lessee. The system is operated by insurance company Acquis.

#Risk

M

Maintenance

Lessees will usually be required to service or maintain leased assets to keep them in good condition.

The lease might stipulate that the service or maintenance should be provided by the equipment manufacturer, or a firm approved by the manufacturer or lessor. For this reason, the period of committed availability of maintenance support from manufacturers may impact the expected useful life of the equipment.

Some lessors will collect maintenance charges alongside the equipment rental and pass these on to the relevant provider.

#Assets #Contracts

Managed Equipment Service (MES)

In the NHS, the outsourcing of the ownership and operation of medical equipment, such as imaging systems for radiology, to a third party. The provider is likely to have contracts with multiple NHS Trusts, enabling it to achieve economies of scale. Where used, MES arrangements mean that the potential lessee is the MES provider, rather than the Trust.

#Public sector

Manufacturer buy-back

See Buy-back.

#Assets

Margin

A lessor's profit margin is equal to its Gross interest margin less its operating expense less its cost of risk.

#Accounting #Operations

Marine mortgage

Asset based lending secured on leisure craft and commercial marine vessels. It is an example of asset-based finance and a Chattel mortgage.

#Products

Market rental

The lease price that would be agreed by unconnected ('arms-length') lessors and lessees. It is essentially a test of reasonableness that is used in accounting and taxation.

For lease accounting where the lessee has the option to continue to lease for a secondary period at a rent that is substantially lower than market rental, this is an indicator of a finance, rather than operating, lease.

#Accounting

Master lease agreement

Agreed general terms and conditions between a lessee and lessor to apply to leases which may be taken out or drawn down from time to time. It is supported by a lease schedule that sets out the assets that are leased at any point in time, together with any terms that are specific to those assets. This arrangement is more often used by larger lessees who will need to add to or change their leased assets frequently and do not wish to have to renegotiate the main terms and conditions each time.

#Legal

Mercantile agent

Someone with the authority to sell goods. When validating the vendor selected by a lessee, the lessor will want to check that the seller owns the goods or has the right to sell them on behalf of the owner, as the basic rule of law is that you cannot sell what you do not own.

#Operations

Mezzanine

A form of debt that sits between normal debt and actual equity. Holders rank below senior debt, which has earlier rights of repayment and first rights in a liquidation, but ahead of ordinary shareholders. Higher interest rates generally apply than for senior debt. Larger companies may use it to raise finance for major investment projects that may include equipment.

#Alternatives

Middle ticket lease

The industry tends to refer mainly to small ticket business (lower value lease agreements, perhaps less than £50,000) and big-ticket (traditionally more than £20 million). For completeness, middle ticket business covers everything between the two, but it is not a term in such common use and the value ranges are not at all precise.

#Market

Minimum lease payments

The charges to which the lessee is committed under the agreement, including any fees and charges outside of the regular lease rentals. The term is used mainly in lease accounting.

#Accounting

Minimum period lease

A lease that will continue indefinitely until it is cancelled after a defined minimum hire period. The rental payments will usually remain at the same level and frequency after the minimum period. It tends to be used where there is not expected to be an extension beyond the initial term. Also referred to as an open-ended lease, minimum term rental or infinite rental.

#Products

Minimum term

See Primary lease period.

#Contracts

Money laundering

The process of concealing or disguising the proceeds of criminal activity, often by depositing cash into bank accounts in such a way that the money appears to have been obtained legally. See Anti-Money Laundering.

#Regulation

Money market

Wholesale finance markets, dominated by banks. Non-bank lessors may also raise funds by borrowing on this market.

#Funding

N

National Association of Commercial Finance Brokers (NACFB)

Trade association representing a wide range of business finance brokers, including specialists in commercial mortgages, bridging finance, and invoice finance as well as vehicle and equipment leasing. It was founded in 1992 and the British Leasing Brokers Association was amalgamated in 1996. It is run by an elected Board of Directors supported by the Executive. It promotes high standards through its code of conduct, complaints handling arrangements and educational programmes including its broker academy, which is run in conjunction with the Chartered Management Institute.

The NACFB's Patrons Charter sets out how the Association's Patrons (that include most lessors dealing with brokers) should behave. Among other requirements, Patrons are expected to deal with brokers and clients with the 'utmost good faith and with a standard of competence, fairness and courtesy'. They should also exercise appropriate levels of due diligence when accepting introductions. The Charter appears to be an effort to address concerns that relationships between brokers and funders were sometimes marked by insufficient mutual trust and respect.

www.nacfb.org.uk

#Associations

National Crime Agency

Government department that leads the UK's efforts to cut serious and organised crime. If a lessor had any concerns arising from its anti-money laundering procedures it would file a Suspicious Activity Report (SAR) with the Agency.

www.nationalcrimeagency.gov.uk.

#Risk

National Fraud Intelligence Bureau

Run by the City of London Police, the Bureau aims to identify serial offenders, organised crime gangs and established and emerging crime types. Incidents of fraud are reported using the City of London's Action Fraud centre. There is no legal obligation to report fraud, but FCA-authorised firms should have a financial crime policy, and this would normally include reporting procedures. Not all cases are investigated; the emphasis is on dealing with underlying problems rather than individual incidents.

#Risk

Near-prime

Customers with lower tiered credit ratings or minor indications of financial difficulty (e.g. occasional missed payments) but not enough to classify as non-prime. The term is more commonly used in the consumer arena than in business lending. Other customers may be Near Prime or Sub Prime.

#Credit

Net book value

The value of an asset on a company's balance sheet. It is equal to the original cost of an asset less depreciation and less any permanent decline in the asset's value that has been recognised in the accounts. Also referred to as the carrying value of the asset.

#Accounting

Net funder yield

The rate set by a lender where Difference in Charges commissions are used to pay brokers. It is the base point of the charge before the commission is added.

#Intermediaries

Net interest margin

The difference between the interest rate charged to customers and the cost of funds to the lessor.

#Accounting

Net investment in the lease

For lease accounting, the lessor's gross investment in a finance lease discounted at the implicit interest rate in the lease.

#Accounting

Net present value (NPV)

The value of future cash flows calculated using the Discounted cash flow technique.

For a lessor, NPV would include the initial cost of the equipment, the lease payments, and any sale of the asset at the end of the lease.

For the lessee, the technique can be used as part of a lease vs. purchase analysis. More widely, it is used to assess the case for a new business investment, with a positive net present value for the investment suggesting it will be profitable.

The discount rate used for an NPV calculation is critical. For a lessee assessing an investment it may be the weighted average cost of capital, which takes account of the firm's various sources of capital and their tax treatment.

#Finance

NHS Supply Chain

The procurement and logistics organisation within the National Health Service. It manages the sourcing, delivery and supply of healthcare products, services and food for NHS trusts and healthcare organisations across England and Wales.

The Supply Chain Finance Solutions Framework offers NHS trusts options for arranging finance leases, operating leases and loans. 12 lenders are approved suppliers, and Supply Chain offers support to trusts to manage the procurement and use of leasing contracts.

The framework is intended to help hospital trusts obtain good value from leasing with having to complete the normal public procurement steps each time they lease. Use of the framework is optional, and an alternative framework is run by the University Hospital Southampton Trust in which 11 lessors participate.

#Public sector

Ninety percent test

For lease accounting, a measure used in the past to help define whether an agreement was an operating lease or finance lease. Under SSAP 21, if the net present value of the minimum lease payments amounted to "substantially all (normally 90 percent or more) of the fair value of the leased asset" this used to indicate that the lease was a finance lease.

#Accounting

Nominal rate

The interest rate including inflation. Where rates are quoted for leasing, they are usually stated in nominal terms.

#Finance

Non-performing loan

A loan or lease which is in arrears (typically 90 days or more overdue).

#Credit

Non-recourse leasing

This can describe a variety of situations where the lessor's ability to recover losses is limited.

If the lessor's only security is the asset that it owns (for example, there is no lien over other assets of the lessee) the lessor's ability to recover any losses is limited to the repossession of the asset.

In a vendor finance context, it can describe a situation where the lessor has no recourse against the equipment vendor. For example, the vendor is not required to purchase the lessor's remaining financial interest in a lease where there has been a default.

May also apply where there is an intermediate lessor, and the head lessor has no recourse against the intermediate lessor for any losses.

#Market

Novation

Novation is a means of transferring a party's rights and obligations under a contract to a third party. The original rights and obligations are not transferred: novation extinguishes the original contract and replaces it with another, under which a third party takes up rights and obligations duplicating those of one of the parties to the original contract. The outgoing party (such as a lessor or a lessee) surrenders its rights and is released from its obligations in the process.

For example, if a firm (which is the lessee) is acquired by another, the lessor may agree to cancel the lease agreement in the name of the original Lessee and start a new agreement with the acquirer (as the new Lessee) for the remaining term of the original lease agreement. A fee may be applied for this service. An alternative arrangement is Assignment.

The term can also refer to the novation of the order for an Asset. The Lessee may contract to purchase an asset from a supplier. That commitment to purchase the asset could be transferred from the Lessee to the lessor closer to the time of delivery of the asset.

#Legal

O

Off-balance sheet

Refers to a business's assets and liabilities not being recorded on its balance sheet. Under IAS 17 operating leases were off-balance sheet for the lessee but this changed with the introduction of IFRS

16. Under UK accounting standards, operating leases are off-balance sheet, although this will change for reporting from 2026.

Few businesses that lease are likely to have any objections in principle to presenting leases on-balance sheet. The values of leased equipment and vehicles are typically low compared to other (property or non-leased) assets. Even when leases are off-balance sheet, details of the values involved are disclosed in notes to the accounts. The bigger concern is likely to be the extra work involved to prepare the information needed for on-balance sheet lease reporting.

#Accounting

Off-lease equipment

Equipment that has been returned to the lessor to dispose of. It is often sold by an agent or sold at auction. It may also be returned to the manufacturer or supplier if there is a Buy-back provision in place. Alternatively, lease agreements may allow the lessee to sell the equipment as the lessor's agent at the end of the lease and to then receive a rebate of rentals based on a percentage of the sale price. Also referred to as 'ex-lease equipment'.

#Assets

Open banking

To increase competition in the retail banking markets since the financial crisis in 2008, successive governments have looked at ways of allowing new entrants to access data on individual consumer and business accounts. The largest nine current account providers must now allow regulated businesses access to a customer's financial data. Arrangements are in place for the data to be shared securely with authorised third parties.

This is intended to create new opportunities for non-bank lessors. It is seen as helping to overcome an information disadvantage compared to current account providers that have access to the detailed current account data.

Data is only available for sharing if current account holders give their consent. In 2023, it was reported by Open Banking Limited that around 750,000 UK SMEs were using open banking products, mainly to allow them to see data from multiple accounts in one place, but it was also starting to be used to support borrowing.

#Business #Credit

Open-ended lease

See Minimum period lease.

#Products

Operating lease

A lease where the lessor retains the risks and rewards of owning the asset. Indicators that a lease is an operating rather than finance lease include the lease term being for less than a major part of the economic life of the asset, the lessee not having any option to purchase or a bargain purchase option, and the present value of the lease payments being less than the value of the asset.

For UK tax, the lessor is eligible for capital allowances unless the lease is caught by the long-funding lease rules. If the lease is for more than 5 years, term is more than 65% of the asset's useful life and/or the lease payments are more than 80% of the asset's original value then the lessee is eligible for allowances.

For lessee accounting, IFRS 16 and UK FRS from 2026 remove the distinction between operating and finance leases for lessees but not for lessors.

#Accounting #Products #Tax

Operating profit/loss

The difference between the operating revenue of a firm and the costs involved in earning that revenue.

Operating revenue is based on total revenue (see Revenue) but nonrecurring items such as accounting adjustments, are typically excluded from operating revenue.

Operating costs include depreciation for equipment on operating leases, marketing and administration, and the overheads of the business. Indirect costs of lease contracts, such as commissions and legal fees, can be amortised over the lease term.

Lessors vary in how they report interest expense. Some present net interest (interest income less interest expense) as their revenue and exclude interest from operating cost. Others report their interest expense under the operating cost heading.

#Accounting

Operator licence

For some types of assets, the lessee or its employees must have an appropriate licence, such as a driving licence, or an operator's licence which allows the carrying of goods or passengers for hire or reward. Whilst it is not the lessee's responsibility to ensure the necessary licences are in place, the lessor might choose to ask for sight of licences as a form of risk mitigation.

#Operations

Operational risk

For regulatory (FCA and PRA) purposes, the risk of loss resulting from inadequate or failed internal procedures, human error, failures in internal systems, or external events.

Operational exposure is the degree of operational risk faced by a firm. It is measured based on the likelihood and impact of a particular type of operational loss occurring.

Operational risk profile describes the types of operational risks that it faces. The FCA specifies that risk to the quality of service provided to customers should be considered alongside the direct risk exposures of the firm. Operational risk is separate from the risks most often associated with leasing contracts, being credit and asset risks. The regulators' focus on operational risk provides a useful reminder that lessors should maintain a wide perspective in their risk management activities.

#Risk #Prudential

Option

A contractual right, but not an obligation. For leasing a lessee might have the option to extend a lease for a defined period and at a defined rate, or to buy or sell an asset. The option will be set out in the lease agreement.

#Contracts

Option to purchase

See Bargain purchase option.

#Contracts

Outsourcing

Contracting business processes to a third party. A common use of outsourcing providers in the leasing industry is to take over a portfolio of leases from a business that is leaving the market. Some lessors also focus on new business and leave back-office contract administration and collections to a third-party. Outsourcers may also function as a standby servicer for securitisations.

#Operations

Origination

The term used in the leasing industry instead of 'sales' or 'new business'. All new leases are originated, either through direct sales activity or through intermediaries including brokers and suppliers.

#Operations

Over collateralisation

Where a borrower provides security exceeding the debt outstanding, protecting the lender from a fall in the value of the security. Over collaterisation may be used to help sell asset-backed securities.

#Funding #Risk

Own-book

Where asset finance brokers decide to fund deals themselves using their own capital or borrowed funds. Brokers might use their own-book to help customers well-known to them who might

P

Partial exemption

Because the regular payments for hire purchase agreements are exempt for VAT there is a complication for lessors concerning how much of the VAT they incur on providing hire purchase can be recovered. VAT on the purchased asset is recoverable, but the question is how much VAT on the lessor's other costs, or 'overheads', should be recoverable.

A business with both taxable and exempt supplies is considered partially exempt and will not be able to recover all of the VAT on its overheads.

Between 1984 and 2000 the leasing industry had an agreement with HMRC which allowed a 15% recovery of VAT incurred on overheads related to Hire Purchase. This agreement eventually fell apart as many in the industry believed the rate to be too low.

Following a series of tribunal and court cases led by Volkswagen Financial Services, during which the industry called for a higher recovery rate, the Court of Appeal concluded in 2015 that the rate should not be zero percent as HMRC had argued. HMRC's logic was that lessor's overheads are incurred only in providing the financial service, which is the non-taxable supply, and therefore are not recoverable at all.

The industry eventually won the case at the Court of Justice of the European Union, and HMRC revised its position to allow lessors to claim back VAT on overheads based on the share of the taxable supply (value of the asset) and non-taxable supply (value of the credit provided plus interest and other fees and charges). This typically led to a higher rate of average recovery of VAT than the 15% that earlier been agreed by the industry with HMRC, with the level of VAT recovery being highest for agreements at lower rates of interest.

#Tax

Partnership

A business owned by its partners, each of whom shares responsibility for the business. There is joint and several liability, meaning that each partner is potentially liable for the entire debt of the business.

Partnerships may be incorporated or unincorporated. Unincorporated partnerships with up to 3 partners are regulated under consumer credit legislation.

#Business

Payment frequency

Lease payments may be agreed at any frequency but are usually monthly or quarterly. The frequency is a trade-off between managing cash-flow for the lessee and minimising administration costs for both lessee and lessor. Each payment may be due at the start of the period ('payment in advance') or the end ('payment in arrears').

#Contracts

Payment Card Industry Data Security Standard (PCI DSS)

The worldwide Payment Card Industry Data Security Standard that was set up to help businesses process card payments securely and reduce card fraud. In general, lessors rely on direct debit or bank transfers for payment, but some may accept card payments from consumers or small businesses for rental payments.

#Operations

Payout

The point in the process of setting up a new lease where the lessor pays the supplier of the asset. It is also usually the point when the documentation is signed or ratified, such that the lease starts when the parties are fully committed to the arrangement. A key anti-fraud check is that the payment is made to the correct bank account.

#Risk #Operations

Peer-to-peer finance

See Alternative finance.

#Alternatives

Penetration rate

The proportion of equipment sold by a manufacturer or dealer for which lease finance is arranged. The term is more frequently used in consumer finance, e.g. for cars, but is equally relevant for business finance. The FLA reports lease penetration rates as a proportion of total investment by UK businesses in machinery, equipment and purchased software. On this measure, the long-term penetration rate has varied between 30% and 40%, the Finance and Leasing Association has reported.

#Market

Peppercorn rent/rentals

Agreed lease payments that would be due in a secondary or extension period if they have been set at a nominal amount. Peppercorn rents/rentals are used to support the lessor/lessee relationship and to preserve the tax position.

#Contracts

Personal guarantee

It is common for smaller ticket asset finance agreements with small businesses that directors are asked to sign a personal guarantee. This can enable lessors to fund equipment that would otherwise be declined. In the event of the business not being able to pay the amounts which fall due, these then become the responsibility of the guarantor, who has to clear any arrears and fees and then maintain future payments as and when they fall due.

A personal guarantee given by the director is called a director's guarantee, or 'DG'. If it is given by another individual who has an interest in the underlying agreement, it is referred to as a personal guarantee, or 'PG'.

Many guarantees include a wider indemnity as well as just the guarantee to meet the payments as and when they fall due. This can be seen as onerous, especially for smaller transactions.

Delivery-up guarantees are sometimes used which means that provided any equipment concerned has been returned to the Lessor in a satisfactory condition, the guarantee element will not be enforced.

To satisfy legal requirements, it is important to ensure that the guarantor has given informed consent and that they have not been subjected to any undue influence in signing the guarantee. Whilst directors are often assumed to have an interest in 'guaranteeing their business', this is especially important for guarantors who are not directors and funders need to take steps to demonstrate that they have taken appropriate steps to ensure that independent legal advice has been recommended or obtained.

Capping the maximum liability is sometimes permitted by funders, and personal guarantee insurance products are available.

In March 2024, the Financial Conduct Authority (FCA) said it would investigate the use of personal guarantees by lenders, responding to a complaint raised by the Federation of Small Businesses.

#Contracts #Credit

Place of supply

For VAT purposes, the location where the supplier delivers an asset. The place of supply for cross-border leases will determine where VAT will be paid on the asset purchase by the lessor. The rules for the supply of services are more complicated. For transportation assets, the place of supply will be where the customer is based, rather than where the asset is used.

#Taxation

Plant and machinery

For corporate tax, investment in plant and machinery is eligible for capital allowances. HMRC helpfully defines machinery as being machines with moving parts. It includes computers and other electronic devices. Plant is anything that is used in a business but is neither part of the business premises nor an item of stock. This becomes relevant to lessors for equipment such as lighting and heating. See Fixtures.

#Taxation

Politically Exposed Persons (PEPs) Checks

Individuals whose prominent position in public life may make them vulnerable to corruption. The full definition of a PEP is set out in the Money Laundering, Terrorist Financing and Transfer of Funds (Information on the Payer) Regulations 2017. The scope includes immediate family members and known close associates of these individuals. Credit reference agencies offer tools to help identify PEPs.

Like all other financial institutions, lessors are expected to undertake enhanced anti money-laundering (AML) checks with dealing with PEPs or companies they are associated with. The involvement of a PEP is unlikely, however, to increase the actual risk of a lessee, and will often bring benefits from the individual's experience and good-standing in the business community.

#Regulation

Portfolio

A collection of finance agreements held by a lessor. May also be used to refer to the total outstanding receivables owed to a lessor.

For IFRS 16, and UK FRS from 2026, lessees may combine a portfolio of lease contracts with similar characteristics (for example, similar assets and similar remaining lease term) to simplify reporting.

 # Accounting #Market

Pre-Contract Credit Information

A standardised sheet of summary information about the lease agreement that lessors must provide to customers before they sign a regulated consumer credit or hire agreement. In respect of regulated consumer credit agreements, this was formerly known as the Standard European Consumer Credit Information (SECCI).

#Conduct #Legal

Present value

The value of a future payment or a series of future payments, discounted at an interest rate. See Net Present Value.

#Finance

Primary lease period

The agreed minimum term of the lease. It should be in line with the expected useful life of the asset to the lessee's business, and not more than the expected useful life of the asset.

The FLA Business Finance Code states minimum periods of hire should be 'no longer than the expected working life of the assets financed, provided the assets are maintained in accordance with the manufacturer's recommendations'. It goes on state: 'Most office equipment should not be leased for more than five years, and a reasonable period of hire may well be less than this for some equipment. Similarly, most multi- functional devices should not be leased for more than 5 years, where the value of the agreement is less than £100k [or annual rentals of less than £30k).

Typically, by the end of the Primary lease period, the cost of the assets would have been repaid by the lessee to the lessor in full if the lease is a Finance lease or Full payout lease.

#Contracts #Conduct

Prime

The most credit-worthy customers that a lessor can deal with. Tends to refer to businesses with no indication of financial difficulties, although precise definitions vary between firms. It can also refer more generally to leases of Hard assets. More commonly used in consumer than business lending. Other customers may be Near Prime or Sub Prime.

#Credit

Principal

The sum on which interest is charged or fees and charges levied.

#Contract

Private equity

Investment in firms that are not publicly listed, typically by specialist investment management firms that manage funds. Various private equity firms, including Cabot Investment Management and Star Capital, have been active in recent years in the UK buying asset finance brokers and lenders. The firms bring experience and their expertise to the sector, although they typically expect high returns.

#Funding

Probability of Default (PD)

The likelihood that a lessee will not pay all if its contracted lease payments. Research from Leaseurope has confirmed that the average probability of default for leasing is lower than that for other types of business lending. Default rates are low because the leased assets are often critical to the business and for this reason paying the lease is often prioritised over other debts.

1-year probability of default (1-year PD) is the probability of a default event occurring in the next 12 months. Lifetime probability of default is the probability of a default event over the remaining period of the lease contract.

#Prudential

Professionalism

There has been debate about what professionalism in financial services means and how to achieve it. At one level it is about day-to-day conduct of business, including treating customers with respect, transparency and making ethical judgements. Above that, the former Banking Standards Board noted, it is about culture, behaviour and competence in firms and across the industry. The leasing industry's trade associations and other bodies aim to promote professionalism.

#Business

Profile

The pattern of lease payments over the period of the lease. For a 3+33 profile, for example, the lessee's first payment is the equivalent of the amount normally paid over three months, and this is followed by 33 monthly payments. Hence if a monthly rate is £100, the initial rental will be £300, followed by 33 months of £100 payments.

#Contracts

Profitability

There are several accounting measures of profitability. The most common is probably Profit Before Interest and Tax (PBIT). Other options include Earnings before Interest, Taxes, Depreciation and Amortisation (EBITDA) and Profit Before Tax (PBT).

A quirk of the new international accounting standard, IFRS 16, is that it increases PBIT and EBITDA measures for lessees that use former operating leases. Prior to IFRS 16, he entire cost of the operating lease was an operating expense. Under IFRS 16 the interest element of the lease expense falls outside of these measures. The same effects will be seen from 2026 when IFRS 16 rules are extended to SMEs through UK financial reporting standards.

#Accounting

Promissory Note

A written commitment to make a payment. A lessee will provide a series of such notes rather than sign a direct debit or standing order.

#Legal

Project finance

A lending arrangement for a specific, and usually major, capital infrastructure projects, such as a building or road. Security is typically provided by the cash flows that the project is expected to generate, such as rentals or tolls. Part of the lending may be structured as a lease

#Business

Proposal

A presentation of a customer's funding needs in detail (often supplied by a dealer or finance broker) which gets entered into a funders' system for a credit review and subsequent underwriting decision.

#Credit

Provision

An adjustment made to the lessor's accounts, usually to recognise or anticipate that lessees in arrears will default. The amount provided for reduces shareholders' funds and is shown as a liability on the balance sheet. There are two main methods of provisioning:

- Assessing larger agreements and customers individually and making specific provisions;
- Assessing the portfolio and maintaining a general provision at an appropriate percentage of the overall value, based on factors such as age of debt.

Under IFRS 9, the leases for which provisions are applied are said to be impaired.

#Accounting

Prudential regulation

Standards set for banks and other financial institutions aimed at protecting the stability of the financial system. The Standards require the institutions to control risks and hold adequate capital.

In general, deposit taking banks are prudentially regulated, whereas non-bank lessors are not. It can be argued this gives the non-banks an advantage as they do not need to hold the same level of capital on their balance sheets. However a benefit of the regulation for banks is that it enables them to raise capital for lending at a lower rate than is likely to be available to the non-banks.

#Prudential

Public Liability Company (PLC)

The legal form for a company that issues shares to the public and has limited liability.

Many of the UK's largest companies are PLCs. Research looking at the use of leasing by the FTSE 350 (the top 350 companies by market capitalisation) suggests these companies lease only a small proportion of their business equipment, although use varies considerably. This may reflect the availability of low cost finance for many listed companies.

Listed companies are Public Interest Entities under European law (whilst the UK is part of the European Union). As such they must use international accounting rules including IFRS 16.

#Business

Purchase option

A contractual right, but not an obligation, for the lessee to purchase the leased Assets at the end of the lease term. If there is a purchase option, the agreement will be a Lease purchase or Hire purchase agreement, which is a credit and not hire agreement.

#Contracts

Purchase price

The price paid for the asset to be leased, including VAT. It is usually agreed between the supplier and the lessee without the involvement of the lessor. The lessor will want to check that the price paid is reasonable, as if not the asset will provide inadequate security.

Lessors may use external services, including those provided by chartered surveyors and specialist providers, to help confirm the reasonableness of prices paid.

#Assets

Put option

Where the lessor has a contractual right to resell the equipment to the broker, supplier or another party at a specified price, either

R

Rate

The interest rate on which the lease payments are based. It is often expressed as a 'Rate per £1,000'. The Rate per £1,000 is multiplied by the cost of the equipment less the deposit to give the monthly rental.

#Finance

Ratio analysis

The financial assessment of a company by calculating ratios from figures in the financial accounts and comparing them with previous periods or other companies. See Cost/income, Cost of risk, Return on capital employed, Return on assets, Return on equity, Loan to value ratio.

#Operations

Real interest rate

The interest rate adjusted to remove the effects of inflation.

#Finance

Rear-end loading

A lease payment profile where larger payments, such as Balloon payments, are made towards the end of the contracted period.

#Contracts

Receivables

The lease payments due to a lessor.

#Credit

Recession

Downturn in economic activity where the UK Gross Domestic Product declines for two successive quarters. Business equipment leasing is often seen as a leading indicator of a recession, as investment in new equipment declines due to business uncertainty about the future.

The leasing market lost around one-third of its total volume in the recession that started in 2008, and on an inflation-adjusted basis took around eight years to recover.

Following the restrictions put in place for the Covid-19 crisis, asset finance new business fell by 49% in the second quarter of 2020 compared to the same period in 2019. However, it then recovered in the second half of 2020, ending the year down by 23%. The market then grew by 14% in 2021 and a further 6% in 2022, returning to pre-Covid levels in 2023. Part of the reason for the relatively small drop in volumes was the availability of support for new business investment through the Government's Recovery Loan Scheme, which was available through many lessors.

#Business

Recourse leasing

Where an equipment vendor agrees to meet certain obligations in the event of the lessee defaulting. The vendor might purchase the lessor's remaining financial interest in a lease by making the lessee's payments for the remaining duration of the lease or for a limited period. Alternatively, the vendor might agree to repurchase the equipment from the lessor or to sell it on behalf of the lessor.

#Market

Reducing balance depreciation

A pattern of depreciation where depreciation is calculated as a constant percentage of the original cost of the fixed asset less the expected residual value at the start of the lease and less the accumulated depreciation to date. The main alternative is Straight-line depreciation.

#Accounting

Refinancing

Replacing an existing lease agreement with another for the same assets. This may be done to extend the term of a lease, thereby reducing the repayment amounts. See also Roll-over.

The term is also sometimes used to describe a Sale and leaseback arrangement.

#Contracts

Regulated agreement

A lease agreement regulated under the CCA. To be regulated, it needs to be entered into by an individual for any amount of credit, or a sole trader, unincorporated businesses or an unincorporated partnership of 2 or 3 partners

Exemptions apply to agreements made with high net worth individual lessees. Such lessees are required to sign an appropriate high net worth declaration and the lessor should not know or have reasonable cause to believe the declaration is false.

Exemptions also apply to a sole trader, unincorporated businesses or an unincorporated partnership of 2 or 3 partners where the amount of credit exceeds £25,000 and where the Assets are wholly or predominantly for business purposes. Such lessees are required to sign an appropriate business use exemption.

#Conduct

Regulatory capital

The capital a bank is required by regulators to hold. See Capital adequacy.

#Prudential

Rejection

Decline of a leasing application or proposal because of poor credit history, unsuitable asset, or another reason. Small businesses may be offered support under the Bank Referral Scheme.

#Credit

Relationship lending

Where a lessor aims to build such a strong partnership with a client that they become the default lessor for any equipment the business requires. It brings obvious benefits to both the lessor and lessee but is difficult to achieve.

#Market

Remarketing agreement

An agreement by a supplier to resell equipment at the end of a lease. This might be part of a dealer recourse guarantee, or simply a standard arrangement for the end of lease agreements. The arrangement may incentivise the supplier to achieve a high price by giving them a share of the proceeds. For the lessor, it can often achieve a higher price than selling the equipment at auction. An alternative is a Repurchase agreement.

#Assets #Intermediaries

Renewables

Equipment associated with the use of natural resources, such as solar or wind energy. As the assets do not generally meet the DIMS tests, they are often financed using asset based finance rather than leasing.

#ESG #Market

Renewal option

Where the lessee can choose to extend the lease term for a defined period and at a pre-agreed cost. If there is no renewal option, it is the lessor who has the choice at the end of the minimum lease period of whether to offer an extension and on what terms.

#Contracts

Rentals

The regular amounts paid by the lessee to the lessor during the term of the lease agreement. May also be referred to as lease payments, although lease payments would also include any fees or other additional charges.

#Contracts

Repossession

Where the lessor recovers its leased asset following the lessee failing to meet the terms of the lease agreement by falling into default. Any value in the equipment can help mitigate the loss due to the customer's indebtedness.

#Assets #Risk

Repurchase agreement

An agreement by a supplier to buy back assets from the lessor at the end of a lease, also known as Buy-back. This might be part of a dealer recourse guarantee, or simply a standard arrangement for the end of lease agreements. The arrangement gives the supplier any benefits from achieving a higher price. An alternative is a Remarketing agreement.

#Assets #Intermediaries

Repudiation

Where it is clear that a lessee does not intend, or is unable, to meet its future obligations under the lease agreement, this may amount to a repudiation, or breach, of the agreement. Evidence of repudiation may permit the lessor to repossess the leased equipment and to terminate the agreement.

#Legal

Reseller

Firms, other than manufacturers, which sell assets to businesses or individuals. A reseller may be exclusively appointed by a manufacturer or distributor or may sell the products of various manufacturers or distributors. Most resellers add further solutions or services making them a 'Value Added' Reseller (VAR).

Lessors may accept introductions for customers seeking finance directly from resellers or through a broker. Alternatively, a customer may simply have decided to source the assets from the reseller. Depending on its role in the finance process, the lessor's credit policy is likely to include various checks on the reseller. The term is typically used in the IT sector. See also Dealer.

#Intermediaries

Reservation of rights

A reservation of rights letter is a letter sent by a lessor informing the lessee of a breach (or a potential breach) by the lessee of the terms of their lease agreement (such as non-payment, for example) and reserving the lessor's right to take action in respect of that breach

#Legal

Residual risk

The possibility that the lessor will be unable to sell the asset at the end of the lease agreement at the price that the lessor estimated the asset would be worth (and factored into the lease), or that the lessor is unable to remarket the asset if that had been planned.

#Risk

Residual value

The market value of an asset at the end of the lease. A third party can guarantee the value, or more usually, unguaranteed. Equipment may have residual value even if it has been fully depreciated for accounting purposes and fully amortised under the terms of the lease agreement.

There are various sources of residual value data to help asset finance companies, including Glass's Guide for cars and vans and auction companies for other equipment.

#Assets

Residual value guarantee

A guarantee made to a lessor that the value of an asset at the end of a lease will be at least a certain amount. The guarantee may be made by an insurer in return for a premium or by another party, for example a dealer or manufacturer. Residual value insurance from third-party insurers was commonly found in the 1970s and early 1980s. Following tax changes and higher than expected claims it is now quite unusual.

#Assets #Risk

Residual value insurance

An insurance policy that covers the risk of the asset needing to be sold by a lessor at the end of a lease for less than the insured value. Tends to be used only for high value equipment with substantial secondary market values such as aircraft, boats, construction and medical equipment.

#Assets #Risk

Restrictive covenant

A term in the agreement that restricts the actions of a party. See Covenant.

#Contracts

Retail bank

According to the FCA, banks that accept deposits from individuals, 'micro-enterprises' (up to 10 employees, turnover under €2million and €2 million balance sheet) and charities, operate accounts for those customers and provide associated services. More generally, a bank that operates consumer and business current accounts.

#Market

Retention

See Holdback.

#Contracts #Risk

Retention of title

Suppliers and lessors often seek to retain their title to the assets until they are fully paid-for by inserting a clause to that effect in their invoice issued to the lessor.

Lessors will similarly include retention of title provisions in hire purchase or conditional sale agreements, to make clear that title to the assets will not pass to the lessee until all payments have been made.

#Contracts

Return on assets

Net profit before tax as a percentage of the average portfolio size over a period. In 2023, the Leaseurope Index showed a weighted average return on assets of 2.5% in 2023, and Asset Finance Policy analysis showed a median return on assets for UK lessors of 2.8%. In the short-term, return on assets can be heavily influenced (and it might be argued distorted) by variations in residual value of assets for operating lease lessors.

 # Accounting #Operations

Return conditions

The terms of the lease agreement concerning the condition in which the assets should be returned to the lessor on expiry or early termination of the lease agreement, and the logistical arrangements for their return including who will arrange any de-installation, transportation and storage.

#Assets #Contracts

Return on capital employed

Operating profit divided by capital employed. Leasing assets compared to buying can increase the ratio for lessees, as under IAS 17 operating leases are not included in capital employed at all, and for finance leases the capital amount may be lower than for an equivalent owned asset. This effect is removed by IFRS 16 and under UK FRS from 2026.

#Accounting #Operations

Return on equity

In general use, net profit before tax divided by shareholders' funds or the company's net worth. For bank-owned lessors it may be necessary to estimate the shareholders' funds dedicated to the leasing product.

#Accounting #Operations

Revenue

For lease accounting, the lessor reports revenue separately for finance leases and operating leases.

For finance leases, the lessor reports the finance income. The revenue is generally higher towards the beginning of the lease as that is when the lessor's investment in the lease is at its highest, i.e. as the lessee has only started to repay the principal. Under accounting rules, the revenue is recognised in lessors' financial accounts using the actuarial method, or less commonly, the Rule of 78.

For operating leases, the full income from the lessee is reported as revenue usually on a straight-line basis, i.e. the same amount each period.

Revenue from associated services provided, such as maintenance, will be added, with the timing subject to accounting revenue recognition rules

#Accounting

Revolving credit

A flexible loan that allows the borrower to repay and then borrow again up to a defined limit. It is commonly used for stock finance, a form of asset based lending, and Wholesale funding.

#Alternatives

Right-of-use (ROU) asset

According to the International Accounting Standards Board (IASB), an asset is "a resource controlled by the entity as a result of past events and from which future economic benefits are expected to flow to the entity". Based on this the IASB concluded for the new accounting standard IFRS 16 that leasing always creates an asset for the lessee, termed the ROU asset. Its value is calculated based principally on the contracted lease payments over the remaining period of the lease term.

#Accounting

Risk weighted assets

See Capital adequacy.

#Prudential

Roll-over

Where an existing lease agreement is terminated early, and the value of the outstanding payments is added to a new lease. It means that the value of the new lease will exceed the value of the assets.

In the right circumstances this can help the lessee, allowing a business whose needs have changed unexpectedly to obtain more appropriate equipment without having to make a lump sum payment. Unfortunately, roll-overs can also leave less sophisticated lessees facing high rentals that exceed the benefits they obtain from the equipment they are leasing. See also Upgrade.

#Contracts

Rolling Stock Operating Company (ROSCO)

ROSCOs own most of the coaches, locomotives and freight wagons that are run by the UK's train operating and freight operating companies. As the passenger operating companies are awarded franchises for routes for periods well below the useful life of most rolling stock, operating leases are used.

Three ROSCOs were set up in 1994 at the time of the privatisation of British Rail. This proved controversial when the newly privatised companies were subsequently resold within a few years at much higher prices. A review by the Competition Commission (now the Competition and Markets Authority) which reported in 2009 found problems with competition in the train leasing market due to the limited choice of stock available to the operating companies.

The largest ROSCOs are Angel Trains, Eversholt Rail Group and Porterbook Leasing Company and Rock Rail Holdings. The value of their combined leases to the operating companies in 2023 was £3.3 billion.

With the new Labour Government's plans to renationalise the railways in the UK, the future of the ROSCOs is uncertain.

#Market

Rule of 78

See Sum of the digits.

#Accounting

Run-off

Where a lessor has ceased writing new business, their existing portfolio is said to be in 'runoff'. In this situation lessors might choose to either sell the book of receivables to a third-party or outsource the lease management. Others will continue with an (increasingly) skeleton staff until the time comes to 'turn the lights off'.

#Operations

S

Salary sacrifice

An agreement between an employer and an employee to reduce the employee's salary in return for a corresponding benefit, which may include a 'company' car or a personally leased car through an arrangement made by the employer. Instead of being taxed on the salary, the employee it taxed on the 'benefit in kind'. The arrangements can lead to tax savings for both employee and employer, particularly for electric vehicles where the benefit in kind values have been very low.

#Tax

Sale and leaseback

Arrangement whereby a company sells assets to a lessor for a lump sum and leases the assets back. The company obtains funds whilst, at the same time retaining use of the assets. May also be referred to as Sale and HP-back.

#Products

Sales agency

Where an operating lease lessee is permitted to sell the asset on behalf of the lessor. The customer keeps a share of the sales proceeds over a pre-agreed value. The arrangement provides an incentive to the lessee to keep the asset in good condition. A broker may assist with the process.

#Assets

Sales-aid

A finance programme set up by a supplier or manufacturer to support the sales of their products, sometimes through a third party funder but sometimes through their own captive finance company.

The documentation may sometimes be drawn up in the name of the supplier, who will then act as the agent of the lessor. The supplier may sometimes also be responsible for collecting the lease payments and passing the lease element across to the lessor. This can be useful when the supplier is also providing other services, such as maintenance, and wishes to issue bundled invoices.

It is important to meet FCA disclosure requirements for regulated agreements and HMRC rules for the VAT treatment of invoices that combine leases with associated services.

#Market

Salvage value

Estimate of the minimum value for a recovered leased asset. Unlike the residual value, it assumes the asset will not be in a saleable or recondition-able condition. The savage value may be zero or even negative, as it is net of recovery costs.

#Assets

Sanctions checks

Financial sanctions orders may prohibit any financial services being provided to designated individuals, organisations, governments or countries. The FCA expects regulated firms to adhere to these sanctions.

HM Treasury maintains a list of sanctions for UK individuals and organisations. Other governments, regulators and law enforcement agencies also publish sanctions, such as that for 'politically exposed' people, which will require consideration in order to mitigate the risk of financial crime. Lessors may use their credit reference agency to check for any potential matches, however unlikely these are.

#Regulation

Schedule

A detailed list of the assets that are being leased which accompanies a Master lease agreement.

#Contracts

Secondary market

The buying and selling of rights to existing leases or portfolios of lease outside of a securitisation structure. Secondary market transactions can help lessors to manage their exposures to individual companies or sectors. In the UK there is only a limited secondary market, mostly transacted between a few of the larger lessors. In the US is it more usual to find finance companies and investors buying rights to leases.

#Funding

Secondary period

The period of use after the Primary lease period. Some leases allow the lessee to continue using the asset at a 'Peppercorn' rental, payable annually in advance. However, others use a Minimum term agreement and will continue charging rentals at the same rate and frequency.

#Contracts

Section 75 claim

Under Section 75 of the CCA, for regulated credit agreements the lessor is jointly and severally liable with the equipment supplier for misrepresentation or breach of contract by the supplier. With a suitable agreement in place, lessors will pass any claims to the supplier to deal with, but if the supplier goes out of business this can leave the lessor liable for any such claims.

#Regulation #Risk

Securitisation

The process of issuing Asset-Backed Securities (ABS). The parties involved in securitisation are the originator, sponsor, trustee and investor. The originator brings the assets (e.g. leases) that are to be securitised. The sponsor, typically a bank, may underwrite the performance of the ABS, and may combine assets from a range of lessors into a single ABS issue (termed an Asset Backed Commercial Paper conduit). The trustee administers the trust or special purpose vehicle that will hold the assets. Securitisation is used by larger lenders, particularly car lessors, to raise funds for further lending.

#Funding

Security

In general, the assets that are financed by a lessor provide the security for a lease because title to those assets remain with the lessor (as owner of the leased asset). If the lessee is permitted to Sub-lease those assets, lessors will typically take an Assignment over the Sub-Lease agreements.

If the lessor or funder does not own the asset (and provides a loan to the borrower to purchase such asset), the Security may take the form of a Chattel mortgage over that asset.

In addition, Lessors may require personal security of one or more director or owner of the business through a Personal guarantee. Other forms of additional security may also be sought.

#Contracts #Risk

Security deposit

Separate from the Deposit that reduces the amount being funded, a Security deposit forms security for the performance of all the lessee's obligations under the lease agreement. At the end of the agreement, it is repaid to the lessee once the equipment is returned in the condition agreed in the contract. Security deposits are uncommon in the UK.

#Contracts #Risk

Self-billing

Leasing agreements sometimes allow for the lessor to collect maintenance payments as the agent of the supplier. This simplifies matters for the lessee by having to make only a single payment. The lessor will then need to receive VAT invoices from the supplier for the amounts collected on its behalf. With the permission of the supplier and HMRC, the lessor can raise these VAT invoices itself, through 'self-billing'.

#Operations

Self-regulation

Where an industry tries to control its own activities to avoid the need for government intervention through independent regulators or changes to the law. The leasing industry's various codes of conduct, including those of the FLA, BVRLA and NACFB, are all forms of self-regulation.

Like most self-regulation, the industry's Codes have had mixed success. They can be credited with having maintained high standards and the reputation of the industry. Compliance with them is, however, voluntary (firms may choose not to join the relevant associations) and often difficult to enforce (expulsion of a member from a trade association for non-compliance is rare).

Many areas covered by the leasing industry's Codes are also now within the scope of the FCA handbook or the (voluntary but independently run) Lending Standards Board's Asset Finance Standards for business customers.

#Regulation

Service

For lease accounting, an arrangement where the customer does not direct and control the use of the equipment.

It can be difficult to differentiate a service from a lease. Equipment within a printing facility at a large company might, for example, be classified either as a lease or a service depending on how it is operated.

If the company operates the equipment itself, there is likely to be a lease for accounting purposes. If a third party operates the equipment, it is likely to be part of a service, not a lease.

#Accounting

Settlement

See Early settlement.

#Contracts

Shadow banking

The provision of credit by entities that are not banks and therefore are not subject to prudential bank regulation. Up to 30% of total credit is provided by the shadow banking sector, which in its broadest sense encompasses all non-bank lessors.

Shadow banking has been the focus of much work by policy makers and regulators since the economic crisis. It was seen as a primary cause of many of the problems, especially in the US. The main response has been the tightening of prudential rules relevant to banks' lending to non-bank financial institutions.

#Regulation

Shariah leasing

Under Islamic law, financial intermediation advocates the norm of 'risk and profit sharing' in business enterprise. It encourages investment in real economic activities that are asset-based and prohibits pre-determined rates of interest.

Shariah leasing, Ijara, includes Operating Ijara, an operating lease with rental payments and no transfer of ownership, and Ijara Muntahia Bittamleek, where there is a separate contract concerning a transfer of ownership at the end of a lease. The lessor retains responsibility for the leased asset, including insurance and maintenance, during the lease.

#Market

Sharing economy

There is a growing trend in the economy away from buying and owning assets towards paying for temporary access to assets. It is now common to find schemes in consumer markets for the sharing of both tangible assets (bike and car sharing, Airbnb, etc.) and intangible (Spotify, etc.). The outcome is referred to as the new 'sharing economy'.

It could be argued this is nothing new for asset finance. Equipment rental providers have always offered temporary access to assets they have often themselves leased.

As the sharing economy grows in importance in the consumer sector, it is possible that more businesses as well as consumers will stop buying assets outright. This could benefit the existing leasing market, although lessors – perhaps in conjunction with equipment manufacturers and suppliers – may need to innovate and accept great residual value asset risk in order to provide more flexible ways of providing access to assets.

#Business #ESG

Short lease

For corporation tax, any lease that is not a Long funding lease. This includes any lease with a term of 5 years or less, and a finance lease with a term of 5 to 7 years meeting certain criteria, including the residual value being above 5% of the original value. The lessor claims the capital allowances for a short lease.

#Tax

Short-term lease

For IFRS 16 and UK FRS from 2026, a lease with a term of 12 months or less, including the effect of any extension options that might be exercised. Such contracts are still classified as leases and are within the scope of the Standard, but lessees may choose not to report them as Right-of-use assets. A summary of short-term leases is instead required in the notes to the accounts.

#Accounting

Side-letter

The term is normally used to refer to a document that is ancillary to or supplements another contract, such as a lease agreement.

A Side letter can also be a separate (but complementary) contract in its own right, capable of giving rise to enforceable rights and liabilities. The principles of contract law apply to side letters in the same way that they do to other agreements.

While side letters can be a convenient means of, in particular, clarifying, varying or supplementing a contract, they can be problematic. Disputes concerning the terms of side letters often revolve around whether or not the side letter is legally binding.

Sometimes, a commitment to a lessee is made outside the lease agreement (without knowledge of the Lessor). The commitment might be made by an intermediary broker or equipment supplier. There is a major risk factor for lessors if the supplier 'sweetens' a leasing deal by offering extra benefits without the lessor's knowledge.

If the provider of the side letter then fails to provide those benefits, whether because the intention was fraudulent from the outset or because the supplier has become insolvent, the risk of a default on the lease payments will increase and there can also be reputational harm.

Anti-fraud checks by the lessor, including calling customers to check what they have been promised by suppliers, can mitigate the risk.

In 2012 it was reported that schools had been promised free laptop computers by the supplier when they leased photocopiers. Lessors were not aware, and the supplier did not deliver the laptops. The fraud was reported in the national media including on a BBC Panorama programme entitled 'Reading, Writing and Rip-offs'. Several large lessors were involved. In most cases, the schools were fully compensated by the lessors well before the media coverage. See also Comfort letters

#Risk

Small and Medium-Sized Enterprises (SMEs)

Usually refers to businesses with up to 250 employees. The Government's more precise definition is a firm with fewer than 250 employees, and either turnover of less than £25m or gross assets of less than £12.5m. The term encompasses microbusinesses having up to nine employees, small businesses having ten to 49 employees, and medium-sized businesses having between 50 and 249 employees.

There are 5.5 million SMEs in the UK, more than 99% of all businesses. They provide 16.7 million jobs, 61% of all private sector employment in the UK. Around 60% of all UK leasing by value is with SMEs. Excluding big ticket and fleet leases, the proportion is likely to be closer to 80%,

#Business

Small ticket lease

Agreements for smaller assets or for smaller total values, perhaps up to £50,000. It can be uneconomic for lessors to deal directly with customers for small ticket deals, so they are often handled through brokers or suppliers, or possibly online.

#Market

Social responsibility

The ethical principle that suggests businesses should be run to benefit society and not only to maximise the returns to their owners. Lessors' corporate social responsibility programmes might include promoting the use of more environmentally friendly equipment or helping to support the growth of small businesses by offering preferential terms.

#Business #ESG

Soft assets

Assets that do not meet some or all the DIMS (Durable, Identifiable, Moveable and Saleable) criteria. Although some lessors prefer to finance only Hard assets that do meet DIMS, many do offer lease options for soft assets.

#Assets

Soft costs

Miscellaneous expenses associated with an investment in assets to be leased that may be bundled into a lease agreement. Examples include delivery and installation costs. Most lessors will be content to include a low level of soft costs in the lease.

#Contract

Soft loan

Loan at a subsidised rate of interest, such as a zero percent finance lease.

#Market

Software leasing

Providing a lease for software is not straightforward, as it is an intangible asset and one that is usually licensed by the supplier rather than sold.

An option for lessors is to treat the software element of an investment as a soft asset, for example they may fund an element of software as part of an equipment investment.

Alternatively, the lessor may be able to agree with the software supplier for the lessee's licence agreement to be novated, or transferred, from the lessee to the lessor. In this way, specialist software lessors can finance software on a standalone basis.

Software providers may also offer a 'Software as a Service' (SaaS) solution. Although not presented as such, SaaS typically has the characteristics of leasing, being for a specified asset and for a fixed period.

#Market

Special Purpose Vehicle (SPV)

A legal entity established to facilitate a specific purpose. For a lessor this might be the securitisation of an asset finance portfolio. For a lessee, it might be to operate a specific project, for example to build and operate a wind turbine and claim relevant grants.

#Business #Funding

SSAP 21

The UK Statement of Standard Accounting Practice (accounting standard) for leases, issued by the Accounting Standards Committee, predecessor of the Accounting Standards Board, in 1984. SSAP 21 required leased assets under finance leases to be reported on the lessee's balance sheet for the first time. SSAP 21 was superseded in 2015 by FRS 102.

#Accounting

Stage payment

For more complex leases, typically involving a number of assets that require construction and/or installation work, the lease agreement may stipulate that the lessor will pay the supplier of the assets in stages following the commencement or completion of certain events or stages of the construction and/or installation. The method carries added risk as the supplier may fail to complete the project or go out of business.

#Assets

Standardised Approach

For prudential regulation, the default method by which banks calculate their Risk Weighted Assets. Standard risk weightings are defined by the regulator, the Prudential Regulation Authority (PRA). For corporate loans and leases, the corporate risk weightings vary from 20% to 150% according to the credit rating of the borrower or lessee. An unrated business has a risk weight of 100%. The higher the rating, the more capital the bank is required to hold.

SME loans and leases are risk weighted at either 75% or 85%, a measure intended to promote lending to small businesses. As part of its implementation of Basel 3.1 rules, the PRA proposed in 2023 to change this to a single rate of 85% although some movement in this was expected before the rules were finalised. As part of the same review, new arrangements were proposed for 'specialised finance', which could apply to some larger asset finance arrangements, and for some unrated corporate exposures.

Compared to the alternative Advanced Internal Ratings Based Approach (AIRB), the Standardised Approach is simple and requires less data to operate. It fails, however, to recognise the relatively low risk nature of leasing.

Use of the Standardised Approach has two main consequences for leasing arms of banks. First, within the bank, the benefits of offering (secured) leasing compared to other types of (unsecured) business loan will be missed. Second, banks using the Standardised Approach may find it more difficult to compete with larger banks using the AIRB for corporate customers with strong credit ratings, or where the bank's AIRB models are used to attach a preferential risk weight specifically for leasing.

#Prudential

Standby operator

When a lessor sells a portfolio of receivables but continues to manage the agreements on behalf of the buyer, the sale agreement will often require an independent third-party to be appointed. This firm could, if needed, take over the management of the portfolio.

#Funding

Standing order

A regular, fixed payment sent from a customer's bank account, set up by a lessee to make lease payments. Direct debits are more commonly used for smaller agreements, where the lessor is permitted to take the agreed amounts on the due dates.

#Credit

Start-up

A new business, generally one less than three years old. A challenge for a lender is that the business will not have an established credit history. Firms may be eligible for Start-Up loans from the British Business Bank,

#Business

Statutory demand

A formal request for payment of a debt owed by an individual or company. When the individual or company that owes money receives a statutory demand, they have 21 days to either pay the debt or reach an agreement to pay. Failing that, the claimant may apply for a relevant bankruptcy or winding-up order

#Credit

Step Change

The UK's largest debt charity, helping people to overcome problems with debt, including with hire purchase agreements. See also Business Debtline.
www.stepchange.org

#Credit

Stepped rentals

Where lease payments increase over time, usually on an annual basis. Also referred to as escalating, step-up or step-down rentals. This method of repayment can assist customers who are growing their business. However, if the customer is unable to sufficiently grow their business, the increasing rentals may become unaffordable.

#Contracts

Stipulated loss value

A lease agreement may set out how much the lessee must pay to the lessor if the leased equipment is damaged or lost. The contract may stipulate that the loss value will be 'reasonably determined' by the lessor, or it could include a table stipulating absolute values over the course of the contract.

#Contracts

Stocking finance

A revolving loan used to finance stock and secured against it. The borrower retains ownership of the stock unless there is a default.

Some equipment or vehicles dealers who offer leasing options to their customers make use of stocking finance themselves allowing some finance companies to provide both products.

#Market

Straight-line depreciation

A pattern of depreciation, where depreciation is calculated based on a constant percentage of the original cost of the asset less the estimated residual value at the start of the lease. The main alternative is reducing balance depreciation.

#Accounting

Strategic alliance

A partnership between a lessor and a manufacturer, for example where the lessor offers 'zero percent' finance deals that are supported by the manufacturer.

#Market

Sub-broking

Where a broker introduces customers to another broker, not to a lessor. Traditionally lessors have not permitted such broker-to-broker business as it is seen as reducing control and therefore causing additional risk. As a result of FCA regulation, some smaller brokers have now become Appointed Representatives or Agents of larger firms. Most lessors accept these arrangements provided the sub-broker has the relevant authorisations and is adequately supervised.

#Intermediaries #Risk

Sub-lease

Where a business takes an asset on a lease and then leases it on to another firm. This is usually prohibited by the terms of the original lease as it affects the ability of the original lessee (the sub-lessor) to exercise sufficient control over the asset and comply with the warranties and undertakings under the original lease (the asset is in possession and under control of the sub-lessee). It is however sometimes permitted using an endorsement to the agreement often referred to as Permission to Sub-Let or Hire. As security for permitting the original lessee to sub-lease the assets, the original lessor may take an Assignment or a Novation of the Sub-lease agreement.

#Legal

Sub-prime

The least credit-worthy lessees. Tends to refer to consumers or businesses with clear indications of financial difficulties, although precise definitions vary between firms. More commonly used in consumer than business lending. Other customers may be Prime or Near Prime.

#Credit

Subsidy

Where an equipment manufacturer or supplier contributes to the cost of a lease. This may result in a lower interest rate for the lessee or a zero percent finance scheme. It can be achieved through a direct payment to the lessor, or through underwriting part of the lessors' risks.

#Market

Substitutability

Under IFRS 16, if a lease contract allows the lessor to routinely change assets during the agreement, for commercial reasons other than maintenance and repair, this is classified as a service rather than a lease. The relevant rules are complicated and difficult to interpret and apply, but it appears that the IASB's intention was to exclude service-type contracts where the equipment being used is incidental to the value derived by the customer. Whether the Standard achieves that objective remains unclear, as most 'as a service' type arrangements involving assets appear to be captured as leases.

#Accounting

Sum of the digits

An income recognition calculation method used in lessor accounting for finance leases. Also called the 'Rule of 78'. Gross earnings (total rentals receivable less asset cost) are apportioned based on the assumption that the principal is repaid over the term of the lease. On this basis, earnings in each month will be lower than the one before.

The formula used to calculate earnings is based on the number of payments due. Each payment is numbered (1, 2, 3, etc.) and these numbers are summed. For a one-year lease, the sum of the digits is 78, hence the name of the technique. The earnings are then allocated to the periods, with the first being the highest digit (12 for a one-year lease) divided by the sum of the digits multiplied by the earnings. Eleven 78ths is then allocated to the second period, and so on.

The alternative, and more usual, technique is the actuarial method. For operating leases, income is usually recognised on a straight-line basis, i.e. the rentals are spread evenly over the lease term.

#Accounting

Supplier

Any business whose main activity is to sell equipment. Includes resellers, dealers and vendors. Suppliers may offer vendor finance to their customers. The finance may be arranged through schemes organised by manufacturers or distributors or arranged through a broker or direct with a lessor.

#Intermediaries

Supply of goods acts

The Supply of Goods (Implied Terms) Act 1973 and the Supply of Goods and Services Act 1982, together with various other legislation and case law, impose a duty on lessors to ensure that the Assets are of satisfactory quality and are reasonably fit for purpose. This tends to be most relevant to consumer finance where the effects of the statutes are clearest. See also Consumer Rights Act.

#Legal

Syndicated lease

Large lease made jointly by more than one bank to a borrower. The technique may be used for aircraft, for example.

#Funding

T

Tax avoidance

Bending the rules of the tax system to gain a tax advantage that was not the intention when Parliament passed the tax law, often because the tax advantage had not been foreseen or considered when the legislation was drafted. It is often, but not always, acting against the spirit of the law and can involve contrived, artificial transactions. The popular view of what is tax avoidance has shifted over the years, making certain arrangements formerly considered as legitimate appear no longer acceptable.

Unfortunately, many tax avoidance schemes over the years have involved leasing. Most had little to do with genuine leasing activities and have unfairly discredited the industry.

Following successive tightening up loopholes in the leasing tax legislation most tax avoidance schemes involving leasing have disappeared. Furthermore, General Anti-Abuse Rules (GAAR) discourage the development of new schemes and the large advisory firms have now stopped promoting them. As a result, the reputation of the leasing industry in Government has improved, although the leasing tax rules remain long and complicated.

#Tax

Tax-based leasing

Leases where the tax treatment of the agreement is the principal motivation for the choice of financing technique. This implies that the tax treatment is preferential to that of other forms of financing the equipment. In the UK this is now rare as the tax treatment of leases is broadly equivalent to that of other options. In the US, the term tax lease refers to any lease in which the lessor claims the tax allowances.

#Tax

Tax capacity

The taxable profits of a business, against which it can offset capital allowances. If a lessee has no tax capacity, there may be extra benefit in using a lease where the lessor claims the allowances – assuming the lessor has tax capacity itself. The lessor is under no obligation to pass through the tax saving to the lessee, but in the competitive leasing market economic theory would suggest at least part of the benefit will be passed through.

#Tax

Tax point

The date of a transaction for VAT purposes. It is usually the invoice date unless the invoice is issued 15 days or more after the date the equipment is supplied.

#Tax

Tax variation clause

Where a lease contract stipulates that the rental payments shown are subject to no changes to relevant tax rules. In the event of a change to tax arrangements, the rentals would be varied to, in effect, negate the effect of the change as far as the lessor was concerned.

#Contract #Tax

Technological obsolescence

Where equipment becomes obsolete because technological advances mean that it saves money to replace it with the latest models. Leasing assets provides some protection to the lessee against obsolescence, particularly with shorter leases. Obsolescence reduces residual values for lessors.

#Assets

Technology refresh lease

A common selling message for leasing is that it enables the lessee to keep their technology up to date. There is certainly a lot of truth in this, as the fixed minimum-term nature of a lease agreement may encourage lessees to review their equipment every few years and, where relevant, change it. By contrast, for owned equipment inertia or other factors may lead to the equipment being used until it literally dies.

A Technology refresh lease goes a step further than this. It entails a right for the lessee to have their equipment changed, or upgraded, when an updated version is released by the manufacturer. Unlike conventional leases where this would incur early cancellation costs, there would be no extra charge. This shifts more of the technology obsolescence risk from the lessee to the lessor. It is quite rare, possibly because most technology updates are software rather than hardware-based, and software updates would already form part of a conventional lease in any case.

#Products

Technology

An evolving term generally used within the leasing sector to describe equipment such as computers, printers and telecommunications. May also be referred to as Information Technology and Communications (ITC). The term tends to be applied to assets for which technological obsolescence is likely. Many lessors will avoid taking residual value risk when leasing technology, offering only full payout leases.

#Assets

Term

The agreed period of the lease. For lease accounting, it is the non-cancellable period adjusted for any option to increase or reduce that period which is very likely to be exercised. IFRS 16 requires the term used for accounting to be adjusted if options are "reasonably certain" to be executed.

#Accounting

Term loan

Bank loan for a fixed period, with regular interest payments due. It is an alternative to asset finance as a means of financing capital investment.

#Alternatives

Termination fee

The cost to a lessee of terminating the lease before the end of the lease term. The cost of terminating a lease usually comprises: (i) all arrears of payments owing up to the date of termination; (ii) all Rentals that would have been payable but for early termination; and (iii) any costs of enforcing the agreement.

Lessors also may seek to recover their broken funding costs and losses and/or costs incurred as a result of the lessee not returning the asset or not returning the asset in a condition that is stipulated in the terms of the lease agreement. A lessor could face a considerable loss if they waived any or all of the termination sum. Lessors may offer some discount on any interest charges for the remaining period. Specific rules apply if the agreement is regulated by the CCA.

#Contracts

Time order

For agreements regulated by the CCA, lessees may apply to the courts to be given more time to make their lease payments. Applications for time orders are, however, rare, not least because the FCA Consumer Credit Sourcebook and recent Consumer Duty rules requires firms to treat customers in default or in arrears difficulties with forbearance and due consideration.

#Conduct #Legal

Title

Legal ownership of the asset.

#Legal

Total Cost of Mobility (TCM)

A holistic view of the costs of moving a workforce for the business's activities, whether staff are using company fleet cars, their own cars or public transport. It includes the expense of the owned or leased vehicles alongside other costs including time spent travelling, traffic fines and fleet administration.

#Business

Total Cost of Ownership (TCO)

The sum of the direct and indirect costs of owning an asset over its life. It includes the purchase cost as well as ongoing expenses such as maintenance, support, repairs, training and disposal costs. A robust comparison of ownership versus leasing would consider TCO for each option.

#Business

Trade-in

Where a business returns old equipment to the supplier or manufacturer and receives a credit against the cost of replacement of new equipment. If the old equipment has been leased there will be an early settlement of the agreement and a possible rollover to a new contract.

#Business

Treating Customers Fairly (TCF)

All FCA-regulated firms are required to have due regard to the interests of customers and treat them fairly. The FCA provides further guidance on how to treat customers fairly based around six core consumer outcomes. These include, for example, the provision of clear information and keeping customers appropriately informed before, during and after the point of sale.

For regulated business, the FCA's Consumer Credit Rulebook (CONC) contains further detailed rules on conduct of business, hence compliance with CONC must take regulated lessors a long way towards meeting TCF requirements. TCF does not apply directly to unregulated customers, but regulated firms are required to conduct all their business affairs with integrity.

Further guidance from the FCA came through its new Consumer Duty rules that took effect in 2023.

#Conduct

U

UK Finance

The trade body for the UK's financial sector. Founded in 207, it subsumed the Asset Based Finance Association, the British Bankers' Association, the Council of Mortgage Lenders, Financial Fraud Action UK, Payments UK and the UK Cards Association. It represents nearly 300 of the leading firms providing finance, banking, markets and payments-related services in or from the

UK, including most bank-owned lessors. The FLA elected not to join UK Finance, maintaining its independence in representing consumer and asset finance lenders.

#Associations

Ultra vires

Latin meaning 'beyond the powers'. In leasing, ultra vires is most commonly used in relation to public sector procurement rules, particularly for schools. In general, until rules changed in 2024, schools were restricted to using operating rather than finance leases, unless they obtained specific approval to do otherwise (which was difficult to obtain), even though finance leases might have been more suitable to a school's needs.

To avoid a risk of the lease being ultra vires, lessors aimed to provide agreements that are unequivocally operating leases and to obtain written confirmation from the local authority to confirm this to be the case. Since 2024, in defined circumstances, schools may use a a general consent to use finance leases granted by the Secretary of State for Education, reducing but not removing the risk of Ultra vires. See Education and Skills Funding Agency.

#Public sector

Underwriting

The process of determining whether to offer a lease agreement to a prospective lessee. An underwriter decides whether the lessor should assume the risk of the proposed agreement, in line with the lessor's credit policy and the perceived affordability for the customer.

Underwriting typically includes consideration of:

- Identifying and verifying the individual, the business and its beneficial owners, together with the proposed assets for Anti-money laundering and Financial crime avoidance purposes
- An overview of the applicant's business (understanding its activities, reputation and prospects)

- The business finances (including its liquidity, profitability, efficiency and leverage, but particularly its expected future cash flows)
- Its management (their experience, track record, management techniques and style and character, and overall forming a view on their expected future performance)
- The assets being invested in (fit of asset with traditional DIMS asset finance tests, the high-level business case / rationale for the investment, fit of proposed asset with business case, and ESG considerations). Although the price paid for the assets is the responsibility of the lessee, lessors will often sense-check the figures.

#Credit

Undisclosed agency

Used where a funder (often referred to as a Head lessor) appoints an agent to enter into a lease agreement with a lessee on its behalf. The agent will be the lessor under the lease agreement and will often provide services in respect of the asset and the lease agreement, but the legal owner of the asset will be the head lessor.

As the agency is undisclosed, the lessee is not informed of the existence of the head lessor as the lease agreement is signed by the lessee with the agent in its capacity as the lessor.

The term can also refer to an agency purchase arrangement (see Agency agreement).

#Legal

U Unearned finance income

For lease accounting, the difference between the lessor's gross and the net investment in a finance lease. The gross investment is the total of the lease payments to be paid by the lessee plus any expected residual value of the asset. The net investment is the gross investment discounted by the Implicit lease rate.

#Accounting

UNIDROIT

The International Institution for the Unification of Private Law, an international organisation based in Rome set up in 1926, which aims to coordinate law between different countries. In 1998 it agreed the Unidroit Convention on International Leasing, intended to promote the legal harmonisation of international leasing.
www.unidroit.org

#Bodies #Legal

Unincorporated business

A firm that is not a legal entity. Its owners have unlimited personal liability for the activities of the business. Leasing to unincorporated businesses is regulated by the FCA unless the agreement is exempt. All broking to unincorporated businesses is regulated by the FCA.

#Business

Unit stocking

Another name for Stocking finance.

#Market

Universal document

A lease agreement that does not name a specific lessor until a particular funder has been agreed. Brokers or equipment suppliers use it to allow them to secure a customer agreement before necessarily having identified the lessor that will fund it. As well as speeding up the process, this avoids brokers having to hold agreements from (potentially) dozens of lessors. However, for funders, using universal documents is sometimes challenging as they will not be able to sign customers up on 'their own' terms and conditions which have been drafted in line with internal policies.

Universal documents are commonly used for small ticket unregulated leases, although for regulated hire purchase agreements FCA rules require the identity of the provider of the credit to be made clear to the customer.

#Contracts

Unregulated agreement

An agreement not regulated by the CCA. This will be a hire or credit agreement made with incorporated businesses and exempt agreements (see Regulated agreements).

#Conduct

Unsecured loan

A loan provided without the borrower needing to provide any security. Apart from revolving credit such as business credit cards, it is unusual in the business finance market.

#Alternatives

Upgrade

When a lessee replaces a leased asset with a newer and more useful version. One of the benefits of leasing is that lessees can do this when the lease agreement ends. Upgrading before the end of a lease agreement can, however, result in paying for two assets at the same time, or paying interest on interest, if the settlement figure is rolled into the new lease, even if the effect of extending the term is to make the lease payments similar to those from before the upgrade. See also Roll-over.

#Assets #Contract

Useful life

The expected working life of equipment before it becomes unfit or uneconomical to use, assuming it is maintained in accordance with the manufacturer's guidance. The determinants of useful life vary between types of equipment. They could include intensity of use, pace of technological innovation, and availability of spare parts.

In the early 1990s the UK Office of Fair Trading (OFT) identified problems in the leasing market caused by photocopier leases being written for more than their useful life. The OFT noted this was artificially reducing monthly lease payments and distorting competition. To help address the OFT's concerns members of FLA agreed not to write photocopier leases for more than five years. The FLA Business Finance Code was amended in 2012 to require FLA members to limit leases to the expected working life for all types of business equipment, noting that this is generally up to five years (see Primary lease period). Also referred to as Economic life.

#Assets

V

Valuation

See Appraisal

#Assets

Value Added Tax (VAT)

Value-added tax is a tax on consumption. The tax is charged on a product or service each time it is sold unless it is exempt or zero-rated. Interest on credit is exempt.

For leases without a bargain purchase option, VAT is charged on the rental payments, as the transaction is treated as a leasing service rather than a supply of goods accompanied by a supply of credit. For hire purchase - which for tax purposes is treated as having a bargain purchase option - there are two supplies for VAT purposes. The supply of goods happens when the agreement starts, and VAT is chargeable. The supply of credit, being the interest charges, is then exempt from VAT as it is a financial service, hence no further VAT is payable.

The VAT rules that differentiate between supply of services and credit were clarified by HMRC in 2019, following a European Court of Justice decision on a case concerning Mercedes Benz

Financial Services' Personal Contract Purchase finance scheme, 'Agility':

- If, at the start of the contract, an option to purchase price is set at or above the anticipated market value of the goods at the time the option is to be exercised, the contract will be treated as a supply of leasing services and subject to VAT.
- If, at the start of the contract, an option to purchase price it is set below the anticipated market value, such that a rational customer would buy the asset when they exercise the option, it is a supply of goods, with a separate supply of finance. VAT is due on the supply of goods in full at the outset of the contract and the finance is exempt from VAT.

As there is no VAT on regular hire purchase payments, this may make the method more attractive for non-VAT registered businesses that cannot offset the VAT they pay against sales. VAT-registered businesses may find it more VAT-efficient to lease assets. VAT recovery on cars leased by businesses is limited to 50% of the lease rentals if there is private use of the car by employees. See also Partial exemption.

#Tax

Vanilla lease

A lease agreement that contains standard provisions. Outside of big-ticket leasing, most leases fit this description.

#Contract

Variable rate

An interest rate that may change over time based on an underlying benchmark such as Bank of England official base rate. Although most leases are provided on a fixed rate basis, larger businesses may prefer the lease to be priced on a variable rate especially if the perception is that rates may decrease.

#Finance

Variation clause

A clause in a lease agreement allowing the terms of the agreement to change in certain circumstances. The agreement might, for example, allow for a change in the rental payments if there is a change to tax rates or market interest rates.

#Contracts

Vendor

See Supplier.

#Intermediaries

Vendor finance

Financial solutions, typically leasing, offered by asset vendors (which may also be called dealers, distributors, resellers or suppliers) to their customers that is not manufacturer (captive) finance. The vendor introduces the customer to either a broker or a funder. Around a quarter of total new asset finance business in the UK market is sold through the vendor channel.

#Market #Intermediaries

Vulnerable Customer

According to the FCA, a vulnerable customer is someone who, due to their personal circumstances, is especially susceptible to harm, particularly when a firm is not acting with appropriate levels of care. Firms are required to meet and respond to regulated vulnerable customers' needs.

The application of the vulnerable customers rules to regulated business transactions can raise some difficult questions:

- Whose circumstances need to be considered? That may be simple for a sole trader, but for a larger unincorporate business it might involve a wider group of people.
- How relevant are the personal circumstances of the individual to the business investment? One question the lessor will consider is whether a vulnerability could impact

the individual's ability to act in the businesses' interests when taking out asset finance.

As regulated businesses are likely to be working with brokers, the broker's direct contact with the customer is an important way that the industry addresses vulnerability. The broker will identify customers needing extra support and meet that requirement, often addressing the vulnerability without the need to involve the lender. Where information does need to be passed to the lender, the customer's agreement is needed first to meet data protection rules on sensitive personal information.

The most common type of vulnerability is likely to be an individual who has limited financial knowledge. In that situation a good solution can be for the broker or lender to encourage the customer to involve their accountant or another adviser.

#Conduct

W

Warehousing

Where an investor buys the rights to leases in preparation for securitisation of the combined portfolio in the future.

The British Business Bank's ENABLE Funding programme is intended to operate as a warehouse facility for asset finance, helping smaller finance providers to access capital markets funding. The first refinancing under ENABLE Funding was completed in 2022 with asset finance firm Propel, where warehouse funding was refinanced and replaced with institutional investors' funds.

#Funding

Waste Regulations (WEEE Directive)

The UK Waste Electrical and Electronic Equipment Regulations 2013 are based on a European Directive, commonly known as the WEEE Directive (which was under review by the European

Commission in 2024). Broadly, the rules require larger manufacturers and distributors to take back used electronic equipment and arrange for it to be recycled or to arrange environmentally sound disposal. Where such equipment is returned at the end of a lease, the Lender (as the owner) holds responsibility for ensuring compliance.

#ESG #Regulation

Weighted Average Cost of Capital (WACC)

See Cost of Capital

#Finance

Whistleblowers

FCA rules, non-binding for lessors other than those that are part of large banks, which aim to encourage a culture where individuals feel able to raise concerns and challenge poor practice and behaviour. The rules suggest that regulated firms should have procedures in place to allow employees to raise concerns in their firms without fear of being victimised.

#Conduct

Wholesale finance

Where a lessor borrows money from another institution, such as a bank or investment company, to use to issue leases in the market. The funding banks will typically set loan covenants that place limited how the funds may be used and require regular reviews of the funded portfolio.

#Funding

Write-off

Taking an asset, such as the amounts due to be received from a lessee, off the balance sheet, on the basis that the debt will not be paid. The amount written off is charged to the Provisions balance, or directly to the profit and loss (income) statement.

#Accounting

Written-down value

The accounting book value of an asset after depreciation and any impairment. Tax written-down value is the original cost of the asset less the capital allowances that have been claimed. The two versions of written-down value should be similar except where the tax system offers enhanced capital allowances. The tax written-down value will then be lower than the accounting book value in the early years of the lease. On disposal of the asset, a balancing charge or allowance is made to reconcile the written-down values. If the tax written-down value is higher than the accounting value, a tax allowance is available. If the tax value is lower than the accounting value, a tax charge is made.

For most business equipment, capital allowances are allowed at 18% per year as a standard rate. However the Annual Investment Allowance may provide a full 100% allowance in the first year up to £1 million, and from 2023 to 2026 the Government has allowed unlimited full expensing (100% capital allowances) for qualifying new investments. Special rates apply to company cars, for example for cars with emissions over 50g/km in 2024 capital allowances were restricted to 6% per year.

#Accounting #Tax

Y

Yield

The return earned by the lessor on a lease calculated based on pre-tax cashflows. It is the Net interest margin as a percentage of the original investment in the lease, calculated over the lease term.

At a portfolio level, it can be calculated as absolute Net interest margin in a period as a percentage of average book value over the period.

 # Accounting #Operations

Z

Zero Emissions Vehicles (ZEV)

Fully electric vehicles. The UK Government's ZEV mandate sets out the percentage of new zero emission cars and vans manufacturers will be required to produce each year up to 2030. 80% of new cars and 70% of new vans sold in Great Britain will now be zero emission by 2030, increasing to 100% by 2035.

For lessors, the shift to ZEVs is both a significant opportunity and a risk, with more uncertainty over residual values.

#Assets #ESG

Zero percent finance

Particularly during periods of low interest rates, manufacturers may offer subsidised credit, marketed as 'zero percent' finance deals to promote sales. The deals may be provided by captives or by partner finance companies, to whom the manufacturer will pay the subsidy. For consumer credit regulated business it is important to ensure that the Annualised Percentage Rate, including any fees or charges, is zero percent.

#Market

INDEX

All entries are shown with a hashtag (#) label that designates the topic of the item. This is intended to allow the reader to find all items on a topic.

There are 22 topics in total, sorted into six categories as follows:

Business environment

#Alternatives: How businesses can finance assets other than by leasing them.
#Corporate finance: How businesses plan their capital structure.
#Business: All other aspects of the wider business environment pertinent to leasing.

Financial services environment

#Associations: Associations and other groups of firms involved in the leasing market.
#Bodies: Official bodies of relevance to the leasing market.
#Funding: How financial services firms raise capital to finance leases.

Leasing market

#Products: Types of leases.
#Public sector: Aspects of leasing specific to public sector customers.
#Market: All other aspects of the leasing market.

Legal

#Contracts: Leasing documentation including lease terms and conditions.

#Legal: All other legal agreements and arrangements pertinent to leasing.

Operations

#Assets: Management of leased equipment and vehicles.
#Credit: Assessing customers' ability to pay, collecting cash and handling inability to pay
#ESG: Dealing with the risks and opportunities from Environmental, Social and Governance issues
#Intermediaries: All aspects of the broker and equipment sales channels.
#Operations: All other aspects of lessors' operations.
#Risk: Avoiding and managing losses.

Regulatory environment

#Accounting: Lease accounting rules and practices.
#Conduct: Financial Conduct Authority regulation of the consumer credit market.
#Prudential: Regulation of the safety and soundness of financial institutions.
#Tax: Tax rules and practices.
#Regulation: All other regulation pertinent to leasing.

BUSINESS ENVIRONMENT

#Alternatives *(How businesses can finance assets other than by leasing them)*

> Advantages of leasing
> Alternative finance
> Asset based finance
> Asset Based Lending (ABL)
> Bill of sale
> Chattel mortgage
> Credit sale
> Crowdfunding

Disadvantages of leasing
Factoring
Instalment credit
Internal financing
Invoice discounting
Line of credit
Loan
Mezzanine
Peer-to-peer finance
Revolving credit
Term loan
Unsecured loan

#Finance *(How businesses plan their capital structure)*

Basis point
Cashflow
Cost of capital
Discount rate
Discounted cashflow
Flat rate
Hurdle rate
Interest
Lease vs. buy
Net present value (NPV)
Nominal rate
Present value
Rate
Real interest rate
Variable rate
Weighted Average Cost of Capital (WACC)

#Business *(All other aspects of the wider business environment pertinent to leasing)*

Internet of Things
Limited company
Limited Liability Partnership
Listed company

Open banking
Partnership
Professionalism
Project finance
Public Limited Company
Recession
Sharing economy
Small and Medium-sized Enterprises
Social responsibility
Special Purpose Vehicle
Start-up
Total Cost of Mobility
Total Cost of Ownership
Trade-in
Unincorporated business

FINANCIAL SERVICES ENVIRONMENT

#Associations *(Associations and other groups of firms involved in the leasing market)*

Asset Finance Professionals Association
British Banking Association
British Vehicle Rental and Leasing Association
Captives Forum
Consumer Credit Trade Association
Equipment Leasing and Finance Association
Equipment Leasing Association
Equipment Leasing and Finance Foundation
Finance and Leasing Association
Finance Houses Association
Financial Intermediaries and Brokers Association
Guild of Business Finance Professionals
International Finance and Leasing Association
Leaseurope
Leasing Broker Federation
Leasing Foundation
National Association of Commercial Finance Brokers

UK Finance

#Bodies *(Official bodies of relevance to the leasing market)*

Bank of England
Bank of International Settlements
Basel Committee
British Business Bank
Chartered Institute of Credit Management
Department for Business and Trade
Educational and Skills Funding Agency
European Central Bank
European Data Warehouse
European Investment Bank
European Investment Fund
Financial Conduct Authority
Financial Ombudsman Service
HM Revenue and Customs
HM Treasury
Joint Money Laundering Steering Group
Unidroit

#Funding *(How financial services firms raise capital to finance leases)*

Asset-Backed Commercial Paper
Asset-Backed Securities
Block discounting
Bond
Capital market
Club loan
Collateral risk
Collaterised Lease Equipment Obligations
European Data Warehouse
Funding
Gross interest margin
Institutional investors
Interest
Interest rate risk
Interest rate spread

Leveraged lease
Money market
Over-collateralisation
Private equity
Secondary market
Securitisation
Special Purpose Vehicle
Standby operator
Syndicated lease
Term Funding Scheme
Warehousing
Wholesale finance

LEASING MARKET

#Products *(Types of leases)*

Asset refinance
Aviation mortgage
Conditional sale
Contract hire
Finance lease
Fit out finance
Fixed term rental
Full payout lease
Full service lease
Hire Purchase
Lease purchase
Lease with sales agency
Leasing-as-a-service
Lease with secondary rental
Marine mortgage
Minimum period lease
Open-ended lease
Operating lease
Sale and leaseback
Technology refresh lease

#Public sector *(Aspects of leasing specific to public sector customers)*

Capital charges
Crown Commercial Services
Educational and Skills Funding Agency
Financial Reporting Advisory Board
Healthcare Financial Management Association
Managed Equipment Service
NHS Supply Chain
Ultra Vires

#Market *(All other aspects of the leasing market)*

Aircraft leasing
Asset finance
Asset Finance 50
Asset Finance Connect
BEN
Big-ticket
Blind discount
Block discounting
Blockchain
Borrower
Captive lessor
Challenger banks
Circular economy
Container leasing
Cross-border leasing
Debtor
Embedded finance
Ethical conduct
Export leasing
Finance House
Finance House Base Rate
Fintech
Fleet
Funder
Growth Guarantee Scheme
Head lessor

High value leasing
Independent lessor
Interest free
International leasing
Lease
Leasing
Leasing Life
Leasing World
Middle ticket lease
Non-recourse funding
Penetration rate
Portfolio
Recourse leasing
Relationship lending
Renewables
Retail bank
Rolling Stock Operating Company
Sales-aid
Shariah leasing
Small ticket lease
Soft loan
Software leasing
Stocking finance
Strategic alliance
Subsidy
Unit stocking
Vendor finance
Zero percent finance

LEGAL

#Contracts *(leasing documentation including lease terms and conditions)*

Additions
Advance
Advance lease payments
Annual service fee

Back to back lease
Balance financed
Balloon payment
Bargain purchase option
Bargain renewal option
Break option
Commitment letter
Consumables
Consumables
Contingent rentals
Continuation
Co-terminous agreement
Covenants
Default interest
Deposit
Drawdown
Early settlement
Endorsement
Equipment schedule
e-signature
Evergreen lease
Extension rental
Fair value
Fees
Fixed rate
Floating charge
Hell or high water
Holdback
Holdover
Holiday
Insurance
Late payment interest
Lease payments
Lease rate factor
Lease term
Lessee
Lessor
Liability
Maintenance

Master lease agreement
Minimum term
Option to purchase
Options
Payment frequency
Peppercorn rents/rentals
Personal guarantee
Primary lease period
Principal
Profile
Purchase option
Rear-end loading
Refinancing
Renewal option
Rentals
Restrictive covenant
Retention of title
Return conditions
Roll-over
Schedule
Secondary period
Security
Security deposit
Settlement
Soft costs
Stepped rentals
Stipulated loss value
Tax variation clause
Termination fee
Universal document
Upgrade
Vanilla lease
Variation clause

#Legal *(all other legal agreements and arrangements pertinent to leasing)*

Acceptance certificate
Administration

Agency agreement
Agency purchase
Annualised Percentage Rate (APR)
Assignment
Bailment
Bankruptcy
Call option
Chattel mortgage
Comfort letter
Common law
Consumer credit
Consumer Credit Act 1974 (CCA)
Credit
Disclosed agency
Facility letter
Fiduciary
Fixed charge
Guarantee
Head lessor
Hell or high water
Hire
Indemnity
Insolvency
Landlord's waiver
Novation
Pre-Contract Credit Information (PCCI)
Promissory note
Regulated agreement
Repudiation
Reservation of rights
Retention
Sub-lease
Supply of Goods acts
Time order
Title
Undisclosed agency
Unidroit

OPERATIONS

#Assets *(Management of leased equipment and vehicles)*

Appraisal
Artificial Intelligence
Asset
Asset disposal
Asset register
Buy-back
Call option
DIMS
Economic life
Fittings
Fixtures
Hard asset
HPI
Inspection
Intangible asset
Maintenance
Manufacturer buy-back
Multi-financing
Off-lease equipment
Operator licence
Payout
Purchase price
Put option
Repossession
Repurchase agreement
Residual value
Residual value guarantee
Residual value insurance
Retention
Return conditions
Sales agency
Salvage value
Soft asset
Stage payments

Technological obsolescence
Technology
Upgrade
Useful life
Valuation

#ESG *(Dealing with the risks and opportunities from Environmental, Social and Governance issues)*

Battery as a service
Circular economy
Leasing as a service
Renewables
Sharing economy
Social responsibility
Waste Regulations (WEE Directive)
Zero Emission Vehicles

#Risk *(Avoiding and managing losses)*

Acceptance certificate
Administration
Arena Television
Asset register
Bad debt
Bankruptcy
Business risk
CIFAS
Claims Management Company
Collateral risk
Comfort letter
Construction & Agricultural Equipment Security and Registration Scheme
Consumables
Cost of risk
County Court Judgement
Credit risk
Debenture
Dual financing

Due diligence
Dun & Bradstreet Critical Intelligence System
Embezzlement
Floating charge
Fraud
Fresh air fraud
Holdback
Impairment
Insolvency
Insolvency Practitioner
Inspection
Interest rate risk
Invoice fraud
Joint Money Laundering Steering Group
Kickback
Lien
Liquidation
Lumia
Multi-financing
National Crime Agency
National Fraud Intelligence Bureau
Operational risk
Over-collaterisation
Payout
Repossession
Residual risk
Residual value guarantee
Residual value insurance
Retention
Section 75 claim
Security
Security deposit
Side-letter
Sub-broking

#Intermediaries *(All aspects of the broker and equipment sales channels)*

Agent
Appointed Representative
Broker
Clawbacks
Commissions
Dealers
Difference in Charges commission
Distributors
Introducer Appointed Representative
Net funder yield
Own-book
Remarketing agreement
Repurchase agreement
Reseller
Sub-broking
Supplier
Vendor
Vendor finance

#Credit *(Assessing customers' ability to pay, collecting cash and handling inability to pay)*

Acceptance ratio
Administration order
Arrears
Audit
Bad debt
Business Debtline
Cashflow
Collections
Commercial CAIS
Corporate guarantee
Credit line
Credit rating
Credit risk
Default

Default interest
Delinquent receivable
Direct debit
Late payment interest
Near-prime
Non-performing loan
Open banking
Personal guarantee
Prime
Proposal
Receivables
Rejection
Standing order
Statutory Demand
Step Change
Sub-prime
Underwriting

#Operations *(All other aspects of lessors' operations)*

Artificial Intelligence
Big data analytics
Conversion rate
Cost of risk
Cost/income
Diploma in Asset Finance
End-of-life functions
Finance Houses Diploma
In-life functions
Leaseurope Index
Loan to value ratio
Margin
Mercantile agent
Origination
Outsourcing
Payment Card Industry Data Security Standard
Payout
Ratio analysis
Return on assets

Return on equity
Run-off
Run-off
Self-billing
Yield

REGULATORY ENVIRONMENT

#Accounting *(Lease accounting rules and practices)*

Accelerated depreciation
Accounting standards
Actuarial method
Amortisation
Audit
Balance sheet
Bargain renewal option
Book value
Capital employed
Capital expenditure
Capitalised value
Contingent rentals
Continuation
Credit loss
Deferred taxation
Depreciation
Earnings before Interest and Tax
Economic owner
Equity in a lease
European Financial Reporting Advisory Group
Fair value
Finance lease
Financial Accounting Standards Board
Financial Reporting Advisory Board
Financial Reporting Council
Financial Reporting Standards
Fixed assets
Fixtures

Gross investment in the lease
IAS 17
IFRS 9
IFRS 15
IFRS 16
Impairment
Implicit lease rate
Initial direct costs
Lease term
Margin
Market rental
Minimum lease payments
Net book value
Net investment in the lease
Ninety percent test
Off-balance sheet
Operating lease
Operating profit/loss
Portfolio
Profitability
Provisions
Reducing balance depreciation
Return on assets
Return on capital employed
Return on equity
Revenue
Right-of-Use Asset
Rule of 78
Service
Short-term lease
SSAP 21
Straight-line depreciation
Substitutability
Sum of the digits
Term
Unearned finance income
Write-off
Written-down value

#Conduct *(Financial Conduct Authority regulation of the consumer credit market)*

Affordability
Agent
Annualised Percentage Rate
Appointed Representative
Appropriation of funds
Conduct of business
Consumer credit
Consumer Credit Act
Consumer Credit Sourcebook
Consumer Duty
Credit
Debt adjusting
Debt counselling
Difference in Charges commissions
Ethical conduct
Fees
Fiduciary
Financial Conduct Authority
Financial Ombudsman Service
Forbearance
High net worth
Hire
Introducer Appointed Representative
Pre-Contract Credit Information
Primary lease period
Regulated agreement
Time order
Treating Customers Fairly
Unregulated agreement
Vulnerable customers
Whistleblowers

#Prudential *(Regulation of the safety and soundness of financial institutions)*

    Advanced Internal Ratings Based Approach
    Bank of International Settlements
    Basel Committee
    Capital adequacy
    Credit institution
    European Central Bank
    Loss Given Default
    Operational risk
    Probability of Default
    Prudential regulation
    Regulatory capital
    Risk weighted assets
    Standardised approach

#Tax *(Tax rules and practices)*

    Annual Investment Allowance
    Capital allowances
    Carry forward
    Corporate interest restriction rules
    Corporation tax
    Deferred taxation
    Direct tax
    Double-dip lease
    Economic owner
    Enhanced capital allowances
    Fittings
    Fixtures
    Foreign Exchange Tax Compliance Act
    Hire Purchase
    HM Revenue & Customs
    Long funding lease
    Operating lease
    Partial exemption
    Place of supply
    Plant and machinery

Salary sacrifice
Short lease
Tax avoidance
Tax capacity
Tax point
Tax variation clause
Tax-based leasing
Value Added Tax
Written-down value

#Regulation *(All other regulation pertinent to leasing.)*

Anti-Money Laundering
Bank Referral Scheme
Data protection
Economic Crime Levy
General Data Protection Regulation
Information Commissioner's Office
Joint Money Laundering Steering Group
Know Your Customer
Money laundering
Politically Exposed Persons checks
Sanctions checks
Section 75 claim
Self-regulation
Shadow banking
Waste Regulations (WEEE Directive)

ABBREVIATIONS

ABCP	Asset-Backed Commercial Paper
ABFA	Asset Based Finance Association
ABL	Asset Based Lending
ABS	Asset-Backed Securities
AF-PA	Asset Finance Professionals Association
AI	Artificial Intelligence
AIA	Annual Investment Allowance
AIRB	Advanced Internal Ratings Based approach
AML	Anti-Money Laundering
AML	Anti-Money Laundering
APR	Annualised Percentage Rate
AR	Appointed Representative
BaaS	Battery-as-a-Service
BBA	British Bankers' Association
BBB	British Business Bank
BEIS	Department for Business, Energy and Industrial Strategy
BIS	Bank of International Settlements
BVRLA	British Vehicle Rental and Leasing Association
CCA	Consumer Credit Act 1974
CCS	Crown Commercial Service
CCTA	Consumer Credit Trade Association
CESAR	Construction & Agricultural Equipment Security and Registration Scheme
CICM	Chartered Institute of Credit Management

CONC	Consumer Credit Sourcebook
DBT	Department for Business and Trade
DIMS	Durable, Identifiable, Moveable and Saleable
EBIT	Earnings before Interest and Tax
ECA	Enhanced Capital Allowances
ECB	European Central Bank
EDW	European Data Warehouse
EFRAG	European Financial Reporting Advisory Group
EIB	European Investment Bank
EIF	European Investment Fund
ELFA	Equipment Leasing and Finance Association
ESFA	Education and Skills Funding Agency
FASB	Financial Accounting Standards Board
FATCA	Foreign Account Tax Compliance Act
FCA	Financial Conduct Authority
FLA	Finance and Leasing Association
FOS	Financial Ombudsman Service
FRAB	Financial Reporting Advisory Board
FRC	Financial Reporting Council
FRS	Financial Reporting Standard
GDPR	General Data Protection Regulation
GGS	Growth Guarantee Scheme
HMRC	HM Revenue and Customs
HMT	HM Treasury
IAR	Introducer Appointed Representative
ICO	Information Commissioner's Office
IFLA	International Finance and Leasing Association
IoT	Internet of Things

IP	Insolvency Practitioner
JMLSG	Joint Money Laundering Steering Group
KYC	Know Your Customer
LGD	Loss Given Default
LLP	Limited Liability Partnership
MES	Managed Equipment Service
NACFB	National Association of Commercial Finance Brokers
NPV	Net Present Value
PCI DSS	Payment Card Industry Data Security Standard
PD	Probability of Default
PEP	Politically Exposed Person
PLC	Public Limited Company
ROSCO	Rolling Stock Operating Company
ROU	Right-of-Use
SMEs	Small and Medium-sized Enterprises
TCF	Treating Customers Fairly
TCM	Total Cost of Mobility
TCO	Total Cost of Ownership
VAT	Value Added Tax
WACC	Weighted Average Cost of Capital

SELECT BIBLIOGRAPHY

- An Economic Analysis of the Financial Leasing Industry, Cyril Tomkins, Julian Lowe & Eleanor Morgan, Saxon House, 1979
- Asset Finance Leasing Handbook, Richard Grant & David Gent, Woodhead-Faulkner, 1992
- Elements of Finance and Leasing, Alastair Day, Financial World Publishing, 2000
- Commercial Hiring and Leasing, John Adams, Butterworths, 1989
- Equipment Leasing, Peter K. Nevitt & Frank J. Fabozzi, Dow-Jones Irwin, 1988
- Equipment Leasing in the UK, HMSO, 1995
- European Leasing Handbook, Marijan Nemet, NWB Verlag GmbH & Co Kg, 2011
- Finance leasing: a guide for lessees in the UK, Graham Hubbard. Institute of Cost and Management Accountants, 1980
- Handbook of Equipment Leasing, Richard M. Contino, American Management Association, 1996
- HP and Leasing Finance, D. C. Gardner, FT Pitman, 1996
- Leasing, Brian Coyle, Chartered Institute of Bankers / Glenlake & Fitzroy Dearborn, 2000
- Leasing, David Wainman, Sweet & Maxwell, 1991
- Leasing and Asset Finance, Chris Boobyer (Editor), Euromoney, 2003
- Leasing, Tom M. Clark, McGraw Hill, 1978
- Leasing Finance, Tom Clark (Ed), Euromoney Books, 1990
- The Leasing Handbook, Derek R. Soper & Ewen Cameron, McGraw-Hill, 1999

ASSET FINANCE 50

The following data is taken from the ninth edition of the Asset Finance 50 (AF50) rankings survey published by Asset Finance Policy and Asset Finance Connect (AFC).

It aims to include the top 50 UK business equipment and fleet lessors based on the latest available data at May 2024. It is estimated the Asset Finance 50 includes between 90% and 95% of the total market.

It excludes some automotive lessors (for example Ford Credit, Volkswagen Financial Services) that do not report separately their business and consumer lending, and some lessors (for example HP and Dell) do not publish separate UK accounts for their financial services arms. Train lessors are shown in the leasing groups table only.

The rankings are based on the lessor's net investment in business equipment leasing. It includes all asset finance agreements where the asset is owned by the lessor during the life of the agreement.

For finance leases and hire purchase, the results show the present value of total receivables less unearned (deferred) income and impairments.

For operating leases, the tables show the undiscounted minimum contracted future lease payments. Where there is no operating lease disclosure, the table shows 50% of the balance sheet carrying amount of assets used for operating leases as a proxy for the minimum contracted future lease payments.

The total net investment in leasing for the top 50 firms was £44.5 billion. Since 2018, the compound annual growth was 4.8%.

ASSET FINANCE 50
TOP LEASING COMPANIES BY NET INVESTMENT IN LEASING

Rank	Name	£m
1	Lombard	6,807
2	HSBC	3,386
3	Close Brothers	3,217
4	BNP Paribas	2,701
5	Novuna	2,463
6	Aldermore	1,779
7	Lex	1,719
8	Alphabet	1,508
9	DLL	1,499
10	PEAC	1,376
11	LeasePlan	1,324
12	Siemens	1,218
13	Investec	1,216
14	Societe Generale	1,198
15	ALD	1,113
16	Arval UK	934
17	Virgin Money	856
18	PACCAR	744
19	Scania	705
20	VFS	688
21	Paragon Bank	644
23	Haydock	601
22	Propel	509
24	Simply	477
25	Kion	434
26	NIIB	397
27	Hampshire Trust	382
28	United Trust	381

29	Caterpillar	365
30	Allica Bank	302
31	Metro Bank	297
32	Deutsche Leasing	288
33	BLME	256
34	Grenke	239
35	Interbay	220
36	Xerox Finance	212
37	Arkle Finance	205
38	Shawbrook	178
39	TP Leasing	159
40	Praetura	154
41	White Oak Europe	153
42	Shire Leasing	147
43	Conister Bank	137
44	Renasissance	134
45	Cambridge and Counties Bank	132
46	CHG Meridian	124
47	Ricoh Capital	120
48	Star Asset Finance	116
49	PCF Bank[1]	107
50	Asset Alliance	101

1 PCF Bank's book was in rundown following the bank ceasing trading Details of the methodology and limitations of the survey are shown in the latest full report available from the Asset Finance Connect website *(www.assetfinanceconnect.com)*

ASSET FINANCE 50
TOP LEASING GROUPS BY NET INVESTMENT IN LEASING AND OTHER ASSET FINANCE

Rank	Name	£m
1	NatWest	10,461
2	Lloyds	6,702
3	HSBC	4,279
4	BNP Paribas	3,878
5	Société Générale	3,839
6	Close Brothers	3,309
7	Novuna	2,919
8	DLL	1,866
9	Aldermore	1,779
10	Siemens	1,710
11	Alphabet	1,528
12	PEAC	1,376
13	Eversholt	1,284
14	Porterbrook	1,263
15	Investec	1,216
16	Angel Trains	926
17	Virgin Money	856
18	Scania	829
19	VFS	814
20	Paragon Bank	793

Details of the methodology and limitations of the survey are shown in the latest full report available from the Asset Finance Connect website *(www.assetfinanceconnect.com)*

REQUEST FOR INPUT

Any suggestions for improvements to the terms covered and additional terms that could be included in future editions would be welcome.

Please contact Julian Rose at *Julian@assetfinancepolicy.co.uk*

ABOUT THE AUTHORS

Julian Rose is the founder and director of Asset Finance Policy Limited, an independent consultancy serving the UK asset finance industry.

From 2008 to 2014 he was Head of Asset Finance at the Finance & Leasing Association. His previous experience spans regulation (Financial Reporting Council, Competition Commission), management consulting (PwC, KPMG) and industry (NCR, United Parcel Service). He is a Chartered Management Accountant and has an MSc in Management (Boston University & Ben Gurion University) and MA in Competition and Regulation (University of East Anglia).

Established in March 2014, Asset Finance Policy has supported more than 200 clients ranging from sole trader asset finance brokers to European banks.

Asset Finance Policy prepares the annual Asset Finance 50 and Asset Finance Europe 50 ranking surveys of the industry published by Asset Finance Connect and provides a range of other data and reports for the asset finance industry. *www.assetfinancepolicy.co.uk*

Stephen Bassett is a Master of Business Administration (MBA) and holds a Finance House Diploma (FHD).

He received his education at Queens Royal College Trinidad and at Harrow County School for Boys.

Alongside his work career, Stephen joined the Royal Naval Reserve as a junior rate and served for many years, obtaining a Queen's Commission. He reached the rank of Lieutenant Commander and was awarded the Reserve Decoration.

Over a span of more than 50 years, Stephen held senior positions at a variety of financial institutions (particularly in asset finance and leasing) including Schroder Leasing, Lloyds & Scottish, Lombard Finance, First National, Broadcastle, Wyse Leasing and Arkle Finance. Much of this time was at Board Director level and latterly as Managing Director.

He currently holds various non-executive positions in the industry and is a Trustee of The Captains Fund (a Reservist charity) at HMS President and previously, was a founder, then Chair and Trustee of AFPA Trust (a Lending sector charity). He is Chairperson for the Guild of Business Finance Professionals.

FURTHER DATA AND RESOURCES FOR THE ASSET FINANCE INDUSTRY

INDUSTRY FINANCIAL DATABASE

Detailed comparative financial data on 70 leading asset finance lenders

ACQUISITION SUPPORT

Analysis of lenders and brokers and regulatory due diligence

TRAINING

In-person and online options providing overview of asset finance, industry structure and regulation

REGULATORY SUPPORT

Support on interpreting and influencing regulations, including lease accounting and FCA conduct rules

BROKER DIRECTORY

Comprehensive directory of around 450 asset finance broking firms in the UK

MARKET RESEARCH

Published and bespoke research on UK and European business and consumer finance market

CONTACT JULIAN ROSE
WWW.ASSETFINANCEPOLICY.CO.UK
JULIAN@ASSETFINANCEPOLICY.CO.UK
07914 071620